OLD Mr. De Luxe

Boston
Official
Bartender's
Guide

Compiled and Edited by Leo Cotton

PUBLISHED BY
MR. BOSTON DISTILLER INC. BOSTON, MASSACHUSETTS

Mr. Boston Bartender Guide

Copyright ©, 1935, 1936, 1940, 1941, 1946, 1948
1949, 1951, 1953, 1955, 1957, 1959, 1960, 1961
1962, 1963, 1964, 1965, 1966, 1967, 1968, 1969
Mr. Boston Distiller Inc. Boston, Mass.

1st printing January 1935
2nd printing March 1935
3rd printing October 1936
4th printing (revised) September 1940
5th printing October 1941
6th printing November 1946
7th printing December 1948
8th printing September 1949
9th printing February 1951
10th printing April 1953
11th printing December 1953
12th printing (revised) July 1955
13th printing September 1957
14th printing May 1959
15th printing December 1959
16th printing (revised) August 1960
17th printing January 1961
18th printing June 1961
19th printing September 1961
20th printing October 1961
21st printing December 1962
22nd printing January 1963

23rd printing August 1963
24th printing October 1963
25th printing November 1963
26th printing December 1963
27th printing May 1964
28th printing November 1964
29th printing January 1965
30th printing April 1965
31st printing May 1965
32nd printing October 1965
33rd printing November 1965
34th printing January 1966
35th printing February 1966
36th printing August 1966
37th printing January 1967
38th printing February 1967
39th printing May 1967
40th printing September 1967
41st printing January 1968
42nd printing April 1968
43rd printing May 1968
44th printing November 1968

45th printing January 1969
46th printing February 1969

LIBRARY OF CONGRESS CATALOG NUMBER: 60-15939

Printed in U.S.A.

Acknowledgements

APPRECIATION IS ACKNOWLEDGED to Joseph DeSoto, founder and chief instructor of the original Boston Bartender's School and to the many other bartenders who contributed their assistance.

EDITOR

Contents

Acknowledgements	v
Introduction	viii
Drink Recipes—*listed alphabetically*	1—112
Special Sections	
Eggnog	114
The Martini	116
Bar Hints and Measurements	118
The Liquor Dictionary	126
Brandy	128
Cordials	129
Gin	131
Rum	132
Vodka	133
Whiskey	134
Index—Drink Recipes	137
Product Illustrations	149
Decorating Labels	149
Glassware Illustrations	Inside Back Cover

An Introduction to the Art of Good Mixing and Good Living

THE FIRST edition of the OLD MR. BOSTON OFFICIAL BARTENDER'S GUIDE was published in 1935 to provide an authentic and accurate recipe book. It was dedicated to the thousands of bartenders throughout the country and to all others who felt the need for an official source of information for mixing drinks.

Since that date more than four million copies have been sold and to commemorate the Silver Anniversary edition issued in 1960 it was completely revised from cover to cover. Handsome new color pages were included with an easier to read format. Special sections on Eggnogs, The Martini, Bar Hints and Measurements were added together with a Liquor Dictionary and many new recipes. The demand has been so great that this reprint is now necessary and as it is the desire of the editor to constantly keep this book up to date, additional revisions and drinks which have become popular, even in the short time since the last edition, are now included. It is gratifying to learn from the innumerable letters which have been received that this book is considered one of the finest and most authentic drink-recipe books ever published.

Old Mr. Boston will appear frequently throughout the pages of this book. He is a rare and versatile gentleman, everlastingly young and ever ready to accept the difficult role of host. Follow the advice of this joyful and genial friend and there will be many pleasant times in store for you. We know you are going to like Old Mr. Boston.

Rocking Chair Kentucky Whiskey—A Blend 80 Proof 72½% Grain Neutral Spirits ▶

A

Abbey Cocktail

1½ oz. Old Mr. Boston Dry Gin
Juice of ¼ Orange
1 Dash Orange Bitters
Shake well with cracked ice and strain into 3 oz. cocktail glass. Add a Maraschino cherry.

Absinthe Cocktail

1½ oz. Absinthe Substitute
¾ oz. Water
¼ oz. Old Mr. Boston Anisette
1 Dash Orange Bitters
Shake well with cracked ice and strain into 3 oz. cocktail glass.

Absinthe Drip Cocktail

Pour 1½ oz. absinthe substitute into special drip glass or Old Fashioned cocktail glass. Place cube of sugar over hole of drip spoon (or in silver tea strainer). Pack spoon or strainer with cracked ice, pour cold water to fill. When water has dripped through, drink is ready.

Absinthe Special Cocktail

1½ oz. Absinthe Substitute
1 oz. Water
¼ Teaspoon Powdered Sugar
1 Dash Orange Bitters
Shake well with cracked ice and strain into 3 oz. cocktail glass.

Adonis Cocktail

1 Dash Orange Bitters
¾ oz. Sweet Vermouth
1½ oz. Dry Sherry Wine
Stir well with cracked ice and strain into 3 oz. cocktail glass.

Affinity Cocktail

¾ oz. Dry Vermouth
¾ oz. Sweet Vermouth
¾ oz. Old Mr. Boston Scotch Whisky
2 Dashes Orange Bitters
Stir well with cracked ice and strain into 3 oz. cocktail glass.

After Dinner Cocktail

1 oz. Old Mr. Boston Apricot Flavored Brandy
1 oz. Curacao
Juice of 1 lime
Shake well with cracked ice and strain into 3 oz. cocktail glass. Leave lime in glass.

A

After Supper Cocktail

1 oz. Old Mr. Boston Apricot
   Flavored Brandy
1 oz. Curacao
½ Teaspoon Lemon Juice
Shake well with cracked ice and strain into 3 oz. cocktail glass.

Alabama Cocktail

½ oz. Lemon Juice
½ Teaspoon Powdered Sugar
1½ oz. Old Mr. Boston Five Star
   Brandy
1 Teaspoon Curacao
Shake well with cracked ice and strain into 3 oz. cocktail glass.

Alabama Fizz

Juice ½ Lemon
1 Teaspoon Powdered Sugar
2 oz. Old Mr. Boston Dry Gin
Shake well with cracked ice and strain into 7 oz. highball glass. Fill with carbonated water. Add 2 sprigs of fresh mint.

Alaska Cocktail

2 Dashes Orange Bitters
1½ oz. Old Mr. Boston Dry Gin
¾ oz. Yellow Chartreuse
Stir well with cracked ice and strain into 3 oz. cocktail glass.

Albemarle Fizz

Juice ½ Lemon
1 Teaspoon Powdered Sugar
2 oz. Old Mr. Boston Dry Gin
Shake well with cracked ice and strain into 7 oz. highball glass. Fill with carbonated water. Add 1 teaspoon raspberry syrup.

Alexander Cocktail No. 1

1 oz. Old Mr. Boston Dry Gin
1 oz. Old Mr. Boston Creme de
   Cacao
1 oz. Sweet Cream
Shake well with cracked ice and strain into 4 oz. cocktail glass.

Alexander Cocktail No. 2

1 oz. Old Mr. Boston Creme de
   Cacao
1 oz. Old Mr. Boston Five Star
   Brandy
1 oz. Sweet Cream
Shake well with cracked ice and strain into 4 oz. cocktail glass.

Alexander's Sister Cocktail

1 oz. Old Mr. Boston Dry Gin
1 oz. Old Mr. Boston Creme de
   Menthe (green)
1 oz. Sweet Cream
Shake well with cracked ice and strain into 4 oz. cocktail glass.

Allen Cocktail

¼ oz. Lemon Juice
¾ oz. Maraschino
1½ oz. Old Mr. Boston Dry Gin
Shake well with cracked ice and strain into 3 oz. cocktail glass.

Allies Cocktail

1 oz. Dry Vermouth
1 oz. Old Mr. Boston Dry Gin
½ Teaspoon Old Mr. Boston
   Kummel
Stir well with cracked ice and strain into 3 oz. cocktail glass.

A

Amer Picon Cocktail

Juice 1 Lime
1 Teaspoon Grenadine
1½ oz. Amer Picon
Shake well with cracked ice and strain into 3 oz. cocktail glass.

American Beauty Cocktail

½ oz. Orange Juice
½ oz. Grenadine
½ oz. Dry Vermouth
½ oz. Old Mr. Boston Five Star Brandy
¼ Teaspoon Old Mr. Boston Creme de Menthe (white)
Shake well with cracked ice and strain into 3 oz. cocktail glass and top with a little Port Wine.

American Grog

1 Lump of Sugar
Juice ¼ Lemon
1½ oz. Old Mr. Boston Imported Rum
Fill hot whiskey glass with hot water and stir.

Angel's Delight

¼ oz. Grenadine
¼ oz. Triple Sec
¼ oz. Creme de Yvette
¼ oz. Fresh Cream
Pour carefully, in order given, into Pousse Café glass, so that each ingredient floats on preceding one.

Angel's Kiss

¼ oz. Old Mr. Boston Creme de Cacao
¼ oz. Creme de Yvette
¼ oz. Old Mr. Boston Five Star Brandy
¼ oz. Sweet Cream
Pour ingredients carefully, in order given, so that they do not mix. Use Pousse Café glass.

Angel's Tip

¾ oz. Old Mr. Boston Creme de Cacao
¼ oz. Sweet Cream
Float cream and insert toothpick in cherry and put on top. Use Pousse Café glass.

Angel's Wing

⅓ oz. Old Mr. Boston Creme de Cacao
⅓ oz. Old Mr. Boston Five Star Brandy
⅓ oz. Sweet Cream
Pour ingredients carefully, in order given, so that they do not mix. Use Pousse Café glass.

Apple Blow Fizz

White of 1 Egg
Juice ½ Lemon
1 Teaspoon Powdered Sugar
2 oz. Apple Brandy
Shake well with cracked ice and strain into 8 oz. highball glass. Fill with carbonated water.

A

APPLE BRANDY COCKTAIL

1½ oz. Apple Brandy
1 Teaspoon Grenadine
1 Teaspoon Lemon Juice
Shake well with cracked ice and strain into 3 oz. cocktail glass.

APPLE BRANDY HIGHBALL

1 Cube of Ice
2 oz. Apple Brandy
Fill 8 oz. highball glass with ginger ale or carbonated water. Add twist of lemon peel, if desired, and stir.

APPLE BRANDY RICKEY

1 Cube of Ice
Juice of ½ Lime
1½ oz. Apple Brandy
Fill 8 oz. highball glass with carbonated water and stir. Leave lime in glass.

APPLE BRANDY SOUR

Juice ½ Lemon
½ Teaspoon Powdered Sugar
2 oz. Apple Brandy
Shake well with cracked ice and strain into 6 oz. sour glass. Decorate with a half-slice of lemon and a cherry.

APPLE PIE COCKTAIL

¾ oz. Old Mr. Boston Imported Rum
¾ oz. Sweet Vermouth
1 Teaspoon Old Mr. Boston Apricot Flavored Brandy
½ Teaspoon Grenadine
1 Teaspoon Lemon Juice
Shake well with cracked ice and strain into 3 oz. cocktail glass.

APRICOT BRANDY RICKEY

1 Cube of Ice
Juice of ½ Lime
2 oz. Old Mr. Boston Apricot Flavored Brandy
Fill 8 oz. highball glass with carbonated water and stir. Leave lime in glass.

APRICOT COCKTAIL

Juice of ¼ Lemon
Juice of ¼ Orange
1½ oz. Old Mr. Boston Apricot Flavored Brandy
1 Teaspoon Old Mr. Boston Dry Gin
Shake well with cracked ice and strain into 3 oz. cocktail glass.

APRICOT COOLER

Into 12 oz. Tom Collins glass, put:
½ Teaspoon Powdered Sugar
2 oz. Carbonated Water
Stir and fill glass with cracked ice and add:
2 oz. Old Mr. Boston Apricot Flavored Brandy
Fill with carbonated water or ginger ale and stir again. Insert spiral of orange or lemon peel (or both) and dangle end over rim of glass.

APRICOT FIZZ

Juice ½ Lemon
Juice ½ Lime
1 Teaspoon Powdered Sugar
2 oz. Old Mr. Boston Apricot Flavored Brandy
Shake well with cracked ice and strain into 7 oz. highball glass. Fill with carbonated water.

B & B

½ oz. Benedictine
½ oz. Cognac
Use cordial glass and carefully float the Cognac on top of the Benedictine.

Babbie's Special Cocktail

½ oz. Sweet Cream
1½ oz. Old Mr. Boston Apricot Flavored Brandy
¼ Teaspoon Old Mr. Boston Dry Gin
Shake well with cracked ice and strain into 3 oz. cocktail glass.

Bacardi Cocktail

1½ oz. Bacardi Rum
Juice ½ Lime
½ Teaspoon Grenadine
Shake well with cracked ice and strain into 3 oz. cocktail glass.

Bachelor's Bait Cocktail

1½ oz. Old Mr. Boston Dry Gin
White of 1 Egg
1 Dash Orange Bitters
½ Teaspoon Grenadine
Shake well with cracked ice and strain into 4 oz. cocktail glass.

Baltimore Bracer Cocktail

1 oz. Old Mr. Boston Anisette
1 oz. Old Mr. Boston Five Star Brandy
White of 1 Egg
Shake well with cracked ice and strain into 4 oz. cocktail glass.

Baltimore Eggnog

1 Egg
1 Teaspoon Powdered Sugar
1 oz. Old Mr. Boston Five Star Brandy
1 oz. Jamaica Rum
1 oz. Madeira Wine
Fill glass with milk, shake well with cracked ice and strain into 12 oz. Tom Collins glass. Grate nutmeg on top.

Bamboo Cocktail

1½ oz. Sherry Wine
¾ oz. Dry Vermouth
1 Dash Orange Bitters
Stir well with cracked ice and strain into 3 oz. cocktail glass.

B

Banana Daiquiri

Same as Frozen Daiquiri Cocktail on page 39, except add 1 sliced medium size ripe banana.

Banana Punch

2 oz. Old Mr. Boston Vodka
¼ oz. Old Mr. Boston Apricot Flavored Brandy
Juice ½ Lime
Pour into 12 oz. Tom Collins glass filled with crushed ice. Add carbonated water and top with sprigs of mint.

Barbary Coast Cocktail

½ oz. Old Mr. Boston Dry Gin
½ oz. Old Mr. Boston Imported Rum
½ oz. Old Mr. Boston Creme de Cacao
½ oz. Old Mr. Boston Scotch Whisky
½ oz. Sweet Cream
Shake well with cracked ice and strain into 4 oz. cocktail glass.

Baron Cocktail

½ oz. Dry Vermouth
1½ oz. Old Mr. Boston Dry Gin
1½ Teaspoons Curacao
½ Teaspoon Sweet Vermouth
Stir well with cracked ice and strain into 3 oz. cocktail glass. Add twist of lemon peel and drop in glass.

Beadlestone Cocktail

1¼ oz. Dry Vermouth
1¼ oz. Old Mr. Boston Scotch Whisky
Stir well with cracked ice and strain into 3 oz. cocktail glass.

Beals Cocktail

1½ oz. Old Mr. Boston Scotch Whisky
½ oz. Dry Vermouth
½ oz. Sweet Vermouth
Stir well with cracked ice and strain into 3 oz. cocktail glass.

Beauty Spot Cocktail

1 Teaspoon Orange Juice
½ oz. Sweet Vermouth
½ oz. Dry Vermouth
1 oz. Old Mr. Boston Dry Gin
Shake well with cracked ice and strain into 3 oz. cocktail glass, with a dash of grenadine in bottom of glass.

Belmont Cocktail

2 oz. Old Mr. Boston Dry Gin
1 Teaspoon Raspberry Syrup
¾ oz. Sweet Cream
Shake well with cracked ice and strain into 4 oz. cocktail glass.

Bennett Cocktail

Juice of ½ Lime
1½ oz. Old Mr. Boston Dry Gin
½ Teaspoon Powdered Sugar
2 Dashes Orange Bitters
Shake well with cracked ice and strain into 3 oz. cocktail glass.

80 Proof 100% Grain Neutral Spirits

B

Bermuda Bouquet

Juice ¼ Orange
Juice ½ Lemon
1 Teaspoon Powdered Sugar
1½ oz. Old Mr. Boston Dry Gin
1 oz. Old Mr. Boston Apricot Flavored Brandy
1 Teaspoon Grenadine
½ Teaspoon Curacao
Shake well with cracked ice and strain into 8 oz. highball glass.

Bermuda Highball

1 Cube of Ice
¾ oz. Old Mr. Boston Dry Gin
¾ oz. Old Mr. Boston Five Star Brandy
¾ oz. Dry Vermouth
Fill 8 oz. highball glass with ginger ale or carbonated water. Add twist of lemon peel, if desired, and stir.

Bermuda Rose Cocktail

1¼ oz. Old Mr. Boston Dry Gin
¼ oz. Old Mr. Boston Apricot Flavored Brandy
¼ oz. Grenadine
Shake well with cracked ice and strain into 3 oz. cocktail glass.

Between the Sheets Cocktail

Juice ¼ Lemon
½ oz. Old Mr. Boston Five Star Brandy
½ oz. Triple Sec
½ oz. Old Mr. Boston Imported Rum
Shake well with cracked ice and strain into 3 oz. cocktail glass.

Biffy Cocktail

Juice of ½ Lemon
½ oz. Swedish Punch
1½ oz. Old Mr. Boston Dry Gin
Shake well with cracked ice and strain into 3 oz. cocktail glass.

Bijou Cocktail

¾ oz. Old Mr. Boston Dry Gin
¾ oz. Green Chartreuse
¾ oz. Sweet Vermouth
1 Dash Orange Bitters
Stir well with cracked ice and strain into 3 oz. cocktail glass. Add cherry on top.

Billy Taylor

Juice ½ Lime
2 Cubes of Ice
2 oz. Old Mr. Boston Dry Gin
Fill 12 oz. Tom Collins glass with carbonated water and stir gently.

Bird of Paradise Fizz

Juice ½ Lemon
1 Teaspoon Powdered Sugar
White of 1 Egg
1 Teaspoon Grenadine
2 oz. Old Mr. Boston Dry Gin
Shake well with cracked ice and strain into 8 oz. highball glass. Fill with carbonated water.

Bishop

Juice ¼ Lemon
Juice ¼ Orange
1 Teaspoon Powdered Sugar
Shake well with cracked ice and strain into 8 oz. highball glass. Add cube of ice, fill with Burgundy and stir well. Decorate with fruits.

B

Bitters Highball

1 Cube of Ice
¾ oz. Bitters
Fill 8 oz. highball glass with ginger ale or carbonated water. Add twist of lemon peel, if desired, and stir.

Black Hawk Cocktail

1¼ oz. Old Mr. Boston Whiskey*
1¼ oz. Old Mr. Boston Sloe Gin
Stir well with cracked ice and strain into 3 oz. cocktail glass. Serve with a cherry.

Black Magic

1½ oz. Old Mr. Boston Vodka
¾ oz. Expresso Coffee Liqueur
Dash of Lemon Juice.
Stir and serve in Old Fashioned cocktail glass with cubes of ice and twist of lemon peel.

Black Russian

Pour:
1½ oz. Old Mr. Boston Vodka
¾ oz. Kahlúa (Coffee Liqueur)
On ice cubes in Old Fashioned cocktail glass.

Black Velvet

5 oz. Stout
5 oz. Champagne
Pour very carefully into 12 oz. glass with cubes of ice and stir very gently.

Blarney Stone Cocktail

2 oz. Irish Whiskey
½ Teaspoon Absinthe Substitute
½ Teaspoon Curacao
¼ Teaspoon Maraschino
1 Dash Bitters
Shake well with cracked ice and strain into 3 oz. cocktail glass. Twist of orange peel and serve with an olive.

Blood and Sand Cocktail

½ oz. Orange Juice
½ oz. Old Mr. Boston Scotch Whisky
½ oz. Old Mr. Boston Wild Cherry Flavored Brandy
½ oz. Sweet Vermouth
Shake well with cracked ice and strain into 3 oz. cocktail glass.

Blood Bronx Cocktail

1½ oz. Old Mr. Boston Dry Gin
¼ oz. Dry Vermouth
Juice of ¼ Blood Orange
Shake well with cracked ice and strain into 3 oz. cocktail glass.

Bloodhound Cocktail

½ oz. Dry Vermouth
½ oz. Sweet Vermouth
1 oz. Old Mr. Boston Dry Gin
2 or 3 crushed Strawberries
Shake well with cracked ice and strain into 3 oz. cocktail glass.

---

* *Bourbon, Blended, Rye or Canadian.*

B

Bloody Bloody Mary Cocktail

1½ oz. Old Mr. Boston Vodka
3 oz. Tomato Juice
Juice ½ Lemon
Pinch Salt, Pepper and Celery Salt
½ Teaspoon Worcestershire Sauce
¼ Teaspoon Powdered Sugar
Shake well with cracked ice and strain into 6 oz. Old Fashioned cocktail glass with cube of ice. Decorate with sprig of fresh mint.

Bloody Mary Cocktail

1½ oz. Old Mr. Boston Vodka
1½ oz. Tomato Juice
1 Dash Lemon Juice
Shake well with cracked ice and strain into Old Fashioned cocktail glass with cube of ice.

Blue Blazer

Use two large silver-plated mugs, with handles.
2½ oz. Old Mr. Boston Whiskey*
2½ oz. Boiling Water
Put the whiskey into one mug, and the boiling water into the other. Ignite the whiskey and, while blazing, mix both ingredients by pouring them four or five times from one mug to the other. If well done, this will have the appearance of a continued stream of liquid fire.
Sweeten with 1 teaspoon of Powdered Sugar and serve with a piece of lemon peel. Serve in 4 oz. hot whiskey glass.

Blue Devil Cocktail

1 oz. Old Mr. Boston Dry Gin
Juice ½ Lemon or 1 Lime
½ oz. Maraschino
½ Teaspoon Creme de Yvette
Shake well with cracked ice and strain into 3 oz. cocktail glass.

Blue Monday Cocktail

1½ oz. Old Mr. Boston Vodka
¾ oz. Triple Sec
1 Dash Blue Vegetable Coloring
Stir well with cracked ice and strain into 3 oz. cocktail glass.

Blue Moon Cocktail

1½ oz. Old Mr. Boston Dry Gin
¾ oz. Creme de Yvette
Stir well with cracked ice and strain into 3 oz. cocktail glass. Add twist of lemon peel and drop in glass.

Bobby Burns Cocktail

1¼ oz. Sweet Vermouth
1¼ oz. Old Mr. Boston Scotch Whisky
1 Teaspoon Benedictine
Stir well with cracked ice and strain into 3 oz. cocktail glass. Add twist of lemon peel and drop in glass.

Bolero Cocktail

1½ oz. Old Mr. Boston Imported Rum
¾ oz. Apple Brandy
¼ Teaspoon Sweet Vermouth
Stir well with cracked ice and strain into 3 oz. cocktail glass.

* *Bourbon, Blended, Rye or Canadian.*

B

Bolo Cocktail

2 oz. Old Mr. Boston Imported Rum
Juice of ½ Lime
Juice of ¼ Orange
1 Teaspoon Powdered Sugar
Shake well with cracked ice and strain into 4 oz. cocktail glass.

Bombay Cocktail

½ oz. Dry Vermouth
½ oz. Sweet Vermouth
1 oz. Old Mr. Boston Five Star Brandy
¼ Teaspoon Absinthe Substitute
½ Teaspoon Curacao
Stir well with cracked ice and strain into 3 oz. cocktail glass.

Bombay Punch

Juice of 1 Dozen Lemons
Add enough powdered sugar to sweeten. Place large block of ice in punch bowl and stir. Then add:
1 qt. Old Mr. Boston Five Star Brandy
1 qt. Sherry Wine
¼ pt. Maraschino
¼ pt. Curacao
4 qts. Champagne
2 qts. Carbonated Water
Some prefer to add the strained contents of a pot of tea. Stir well and decorate with fruits in season. Serve in 4 oz. Punch glasses.

Boston Bullet

See *Special Martini Section* on pages 116 and 117.

Boston Cocktail

¾ oz. Old Mr. Boston Dry Gin
¾ oz. Old Mr. Boston Apricot Flavored Brandy
Juice of ¼ Lemon
¼ oz. Grenadine
Shake well with cracked ice and strain into 3 oz. cocktail glass.

Boston Cooler

Into 12 oz. Tom Collins glass, put:
Juice ½ Lemon
1 Teaspoon Powdered Sugar
2 oz. Carbonated Water
Stir. Then fill glass with cracked ice and add:
2 oz. Old Mr. Boston Imported Rum
Fill with carbonated water or ginger ale and stir again. Insert spiral of orange or lemon peel (or both) and dangle end over rim of glass.

Boston Side Car Cocktail

¾ oz. Old Mr. Boston Five Star Brandy
¾ oz. Old Mr. Boston Imported Rum
¾ oz. Triple Sec
Juice ½ Lime
Shake well with cracked ice and strain into 3 oz. cocktail glass.

B

Boston Sour

Juice ½ Lemon
1 Teaspoon Powdered Sugar
2 oz. Old Mr. Boston Whiskey*
White of 1 Egg
Shake well with cracked ice and strain into 8 oz. highball glass. Then add cube of ice, fill with carbonated water and decorate with half-slice of lemon and a cherry.

Bourbon Highball

1 Cube of Ice
2 oz. Old Mr. Boston Kentucky Bourbon Whiskey
Fill 8 oz. highball glass with ginger ale or carbonated water. Add twist of lemon peel, if desired, and stir.

Brandy and Soda

2 Cubes of Ice
2 oz. Old Mr. Boston Five Star Brandy
6 oz. Carbonated Water
Serve in 12 oz. Tom Collins glass and stir.

Brandy Blazer

1 Lump Sugar
1 Piece Orange Peel
1 Piece Lemon Peel
2 oz. Old Mr. Boston Five Star Brandy
Use Old Fashioned cocktail glass. Light with a match, stir with long spoon for a few seconds and strain into a hot whiskey glass.

Brandy Cobbler

Dissolve: 1 teaspoon powdered sugar in 2 oz. carbonated water; then fill 10 oz. goblet with shaved ice.
Add 2 oz. Old Mr. Boston Five Star Brandy
Stir well and decorate with fruits in season. Serve with straws.

Brandy Cocktail

2 oz. Old Mr. Boston Five Star Brandy
¼ Teaspoon Simple Syrup
2 Dashes Bitters
Twist of Lemon Peel
Stir well with cracked ice and strain into 3 oz. cocktail glass.

Brandy Collins

Juice ½ Lemon
1 Teaspoon Powdered Sugar
2 oz. Old Mr. Boston Five Star Brandy
Shake well with cracked ice and strain into 12 oz. Tom Collins glass. Add several cubes of ice, fill with carbonated water and stir. Decorate with slice of orange, lemon and a cherry. Serve with straws.

---

* Bourbon, Blended, Rye or Canadian.

B

Brandy Crusta Cocktail

Moisten the edge of 4 oz. cocktail glass with lemon and dip into sugar. Cut the rind of half a lemon in a spiral, and place in glass.
1 Teaspoon Maraschino
1 Dash Bitters
1 Teaspoon Lemon Juice
½ oz. Curacao
2 oz. Old Mr. Boston Five Star Brandy
Stir above ingredients in mixing glass and strain into glass prepared as above. Add slice of orange.

Brandy Daisy

Juice of ½ Lemon
½ Teaspoon Powdered Sugar
1 Teaspoon Raspberry Syrup or Grenadine
2 oz. Old Mr. Boston Five Star Brandy
Shake well with cracked ice and strain into Stein or 8 oz. metal cup. Add cube of ice and decorate with fruit.

Brandy Eggnog

1 Egg
1 Teaspoon Powdered Sugar
2 oz. Old Mr. Boston Five Star Brandy
Fill glass with Milk
Shake well with cracked ice and strain into 12 oz. Tom Collins glass. Grate nutmeg on top.

Brandy Fix

Juice ½ Lemon
1 Teaspoon Powdered Sugar
1 Teaspoon Water
Stir. Then fill glass with shaved ice.
2½ oz. Old Mr. Boston Five Star Brandy
Use 8 oz. highball glass. Stir well. Add slice of lemon. Serve with straws.

Brandy Fizz

Juice ½ Lemon
1 Teaspoon Powdered Sugar
2 oz. Old Mr. Boston Five Star Brandy
Shake well with cracked ice and strain into 7 oz. highball glass. Fill with carbonated water.

Brandy Flip

1 Egg
1 Teaspoon Powdered Sugar
1½ oz. Old Mr. Boston Five Star Brandy
2 Teaspoons Sweet Cream (if desired)
Shake well with cracked ice and strain into 5 oz. flip glass. Grate a little nutmeg on top.

Brandy Gump Cocktail

1½ oz. Old Mr. Boston Five Star Brandy
Juice of ½ Lemon
½ Teaspoon Grenadine
Shake well with cracked ice and strain into 3 oz. cocktail glass.

B

Brandy Highball

1 Cube of Ice
2 oz. Old Mr. Boston Five Star Brandy
Fill 8 oz. highball glass with ginger ale or carbonated water. Add twist of lemon peel, if desired, and stir gently.

Brandy Julep

Into 12 oz. Tom Collins glass put:
1 Teaspoon Powdered Sugar
5 or 6 Sprigs Fresh Mint
2½ oz. Old Mr. Boston Five Star Brandy
Then fill glass with finely shaved ice, and stir until mint rises to top, being careful not to bruise mint. (Do not hold glass with hand while stirring.) Decorate with slice of pineapple, orange, lemon and a cherry. Serve with straws.

Brandy Milk Punch

1 Teaspoon Powdered Sugar
2 oz. Old Mr. Boston Five Star Brandy
½ Pint Milk
Shake well with cracked ice, strain into 12 oz. Tom Collins glass and grate nutmeg on top.

Brandy Punch

Juice of 1 Dozen Lemons
Juice of 4 Oranges
Add enough sugar to sweeten.
8 oz. Grenadine
1 qt. Carbonated Water
Place large block of ice in punch bowl and stir well. Then add:
½ Pint Curacao
2 qts. Old Mr. Boston Five Star Brandy
Some prefer to add the strained contents of a pot of tea. Stir well and decorate with fruits in season. Serve in 4 oz. punch glasses.

Brandy Sangaree

Dissolve ½ teaspoon powdered sugar in 1 teaspoon of water.
2 oz. Old Mr. Boston Five Star Brandy
2 Cubes of Ice
Serve in 8 oz. highball glass. Fill balance with soda water. Stir, leaving enough room on which to float a tablespoon of Port Wine. Sprinkle lightly with nutmeg.

Brandy Sling

Dissolve 1 Teaspoon Powdered Sugar in Teaspoon of Water and Juice ½ Lemon.
2 oz. Old Mr. Boston Five Star Brandy
2 Cubes of Ice
Serve in Old Fashioned cocktail glass and stir. Twist of lemon peel and drop in glass.

B

Brandy Smash

Muddle 1 Lump of Sugar with
1 oz. Carbonated Water and
4 Sprigs of Green Mint
2 oz. Old Mr. Boston Five Star Brandy
Add a cube of ice. Stir and decorate with a slice of Orange and a cherry. Twist lemon peel on top. Use Old Fashioned cocktail glass.

Brandy Sour

Juice ½ Lemon
½ Teaspoon Powdered Sugar
2 oz. Old Mr. Boston Five Star Brandy
Shake well with cracked ice and strain into 6 oz. sour glass. Decorate with a half-slice of lemon and a cherry.

Brandy Squirt

1½ oz. Old Mr. Boston Five Star Brandy
1 Tablespoon Powdered Sugar
1 Teaspoon Raspberry Syrup or Grenadine
Shake well with cracked ice and strain into 8 oz. highball glass and fill with carbonated water. Decorate with cubes of pineapple and strawberries.

Brandy Swizzle

Made same as Gin Swizzle *(see page 43), using* 2 oz. Old Mr. Boston Five Star Brandy.

Brandy Toddy

Use Old Fashioned cocktail glass.
½ Teaspoon Powdered Sugar
2 Teaspoons Water *and stir.*
2 oz. Old Mr. Boston Five Star Brandy
1 Lump of Ice
Stir again and twist lemon peel on top.

Brandy Toddy (Hot)

Put lump of sugar into hot whiskey glass and fill two-thirds with boiling water. Add 2 oz. Old Mr. Boston Five Star Brandy. Stir and decorate with slice of lemon. Grate nutmeg on top.

Brandy Vermouth Cocktail

½ oz. Sweet Vermouth
2 oz. Old Mr. Boston Five Star Brandy
1 Dash Bitters
Stir well with cracked ice and strain into 3 oz. cocktail glass.

Brazil Cocktail

1¼ oz. Dry Vermouth
1¼ oz. Sherry Wine
1 Dash Bitters
¼ Teaspoon Absinthe Substitute
Stir well with cracked ice and strain into 3 oz. cocktail glass.

Breakfast Eggnog

1 Egg
½ oz. Curacao
2 oz. Old Mr. Boston Apricot Flavored Brandy
Fill glass with milk. Shake well with cracked ice and strain into 12 oz. Tom Collins glass. Grate nutmeg on top.

B

Brighton Punch

¾ oz. Old Mr. Boston Whiskey*
¾ oz. Cognac
¾ oz. Benedictine
Juice ½ Orange
Juice ½ Lemon
Shake well and pour into 12 oz. Tom Collins glass filled with shaved ice. Then fill with carbonated water and stir gently. Serve with straws. Old Mr. Boston Five Star Brandy may be substituted for Cognac.

Broken Spur Cocktail

¾ oz. Sweet Vermouth
1½ oz. Port Wine
¼ Teaspoon Curacao
Stir well with cracked ice and strain into 3 oz. cocktail glass.

Bronx Cocktail

1 oz. Old Mr. Boston Dry Gin
½ oz. Dry Vermouth
½ oz. Sweet Vermouth
Juice ¼ Orange
Shake well with cracked ice and strain into 3 oz. cocktail glass. Serve with slice of orange.

Bronx Cocktail (Dry)

1 oz. Old Mr. Boston Dry Gin
1 oz. Dry Vermouth
Juice ¼ Orange
Shake well with cracked ice and strain into 3 oz. cocktail glass. Serve with slice of orange.

Bronx Golden Cocktail

Made same as Bronx Cocktail, *adding the yolk of one egg. Use 4 oz. cocktail glass.*

Bronx Silver Cocktail

Juice of ¼ Orange
White of 1 Egg
½ oz. Dry Vermouth
1 oz. Old Mr. Boston Dry Gin
Shake well with cracked ice and strain into 4 oz. cocktail glass.

Bronx Terrace Cocktail

1½ oz. Old Mr. Boston Dry Gin
1½ oz. Dry Vermouth
Juice of ½ Lime
Shake well with cracked ice and strain into 3 oz. cocktail glass. Add a cherry.

Brown Cocktail

¾ oz. Old Mr. Boston Dry Gin
¾ oz. Old Mr. Boston Imported Rum
¾ oz. Dry Vermouth
Stir well with cracked ice and strain into 3 oz. cocktail glass.

Bucks Fizz

¼ Glass Orange Juice
Fill with Champagne. Use 12 oz. Tom Collins glass and stir very gently.

Bulldog Cocktail

1¼ oz. Old Mr. Boston Wild Cherry Flavored Brandy
¾ oz. Old Mr. Boston Dry Gin
Juice of ½ Lime
Shake well with cracked ice and strain into 3 oz. cocktail glass.

Bulldog Highball

1 Cube of Ice
Juice of ½ Orange
2 oz. Old Mr. Boston Dry Gin
Fill 8 oz. highball glass with ginger ale and stir.

* Bourbon, Blended, Rye or Canadian.

Straight Bourbon 80 Proof ▶

C

Bull's Eye

1 oz. Old Mr. Boston Five Star Brandy
2 oz. Hard Cider
1 Cube of Ice
Fill 8 oz. highball glass with ginger ale and stir.

Bull's Milk

1 Teaspoon Powdered Sugar
1 oz. Old Mr. Boston Imported Rum
1½ oz. Old Mr. Boston Five Star Brandy
½ Pint Milk
Shake well with cracked ice and strain into 12 oz. Tom Collins glass. Grate nutmeg and pinch of cinnamon on top.

Burgundy Bishop

Juice ¼ Lemon
1 Teaspoon Powdered Sugar
1 oz. Old Mr. Boston Imported Rum
Shake well and strain into 8 oz. highball glass and fill with Burgundy and stir. Decorate with fruits.

Button Hook Cocktail

½ oz. Old Mr. Boston Creme de Menthe (White)
½ oz. Old Mr. Boston Apricot Flavored Brandy
½ oz. Absinthe Substitute
½ oz. Old Mr. Boston Five Star Brandy
Shake well with cracked ice and strain into 3 oz. cocktail glass.

Cabaret Cocktail

1½ oz. Old Mr. Boston Dry Gin
2 Dashes Bitters
½ Teaspoon Dry Vermouth
¼ Teaspoon Benedictine
Stir well with cracked ice and strain into 3 oz. cocktail glass. Serve with a cherry.

Cablegram Highball

Juice ½ Lemon
1 Teaspoon Powdered Sugar
2 oz. Old Mr. Boston Whiskey*
Stir well with cracked ice and fill with ginger ale. Use 8 oz. highball glass.

* Bourbon, Blended, Rye or Canadian.

C

Café de Paris Cocktail

White of 1 Egg
1 Teaspoon Absinthe Substitute
1 Teaspoon Sweet Cream
1½ oz. Old Mr. Boston Dry Gin
Shake well with cracked ice and strain into 4 oz. cocktail glass.

Café Royale

1 Cup Hot Black Coffee
Put cube of sugar, well soaked with Old Mr. Boston Five Star Brandy, in teaspoon and hold so that it will rest on top of coffee and ignite and hold until flame burns out. Drop contents in coffee.

California Lemonade

Juice 1 Lemon
Juice 1 Lime
3 Teaspoons Powdered Sugar
2 oz. Old Mr. Boston Whiskey*
¼ Teaspoon Grenadine
Shake well with cracked ice and strain into 12 oz. Tom Collins glass filled with shaved ice. Fill with carbonated water and decorate with slice of orange, lemon, and a cherry. Serve with straws.

Cameron's Kick Cocktail

¾ oz. Old Mr. Boston Scotch Whisky
¼ oz. Irish Whiskey
Juice ¼ Lemon
2 Dashes Orange Bitters
Shake well with cracked ice and strain into 3 oz. cocktail glass.

Cape Codder

1½ oz. Old Mr. Boston Vodka or Old Mr. Boston Imported Rum
3 oz. Cranberry Juice
Juice ½ Lime (if desired)
May be served on the rocks in Old Fashioned Cocktail glass or in 8 oz. highball glass with cubes of ice and carbonated water. Stir.

Cardinal Punch

Juice of 1 Dozen Lemons
Add enough Powdered Sugar to sweeten. Place large block of ice in punch bowl and stir well. Then add:
1 pt. Old Mr. Boston Five Star Brandy
1 pt. Old Mr. Boston Imported Rum
1 pt. Champagne
2 qts. Claret
1 qt. Carbonated Water
½ pt. Sweet Vermouth
Some prefer to add the strained contents of a pot of tea. Stir well and decorate with fruits in season. Serve in 4 oz. punch glasses.

Carrol Cocktail

1½ oz. Old Mr. Boston Five Star Brandy
¾ oz. Sweet Vermouth
Stir well with cracked ice and strain into 3 oz. cocktail glass. Serve with a cherry.

* *Bourbon, Blended, Rye or Canadian.*

C

Casino Cocktail

2 Dashes Orange Bitters
¼ Teaspoon Maraschino
¼ Teaspoon Lemon Juice
2 oz. Old Mr. Boston Dry Gin
Shake well with cracked ice and strain into 3 oz. cocktail glass. Serve with a cherry.

Champagne Cocktail

Spiral Rind of ½ Lemon
1 Lump Sugar
2 Dashes Bitters
Use 6 oz. Champagne glass. Fill with Champagne.

Champagne Cup

Use Large Glass Pitcher
4 Teaspoons Powdered Sugar
6 oz. Carbonated Water
½ oz. Triple Sec
½ oz. Curacao
2 oz. Old Mr. Boston Five Star Brandy
Fill pitcher with cubes of ice. Add 1 pint of Champagne. Stir well and decorate with as many fruits as available and also rind of cucumber inserted on each side of pitcher. Top with small bunch of mint sprigs. Serve in 5 oz. claret glass.

Champagne Punch

Juice of 1 Dozen Lemons
Add enough Powdered Sugar to sweeten. Place large block of ice in punch bowl and stir well. Then add:
½ pt. Maraschino
½ pt. Curacao
1 pt. Old Mr. Boston Five Star Brandy
2 qts. Champagne
1 qt. Carbonated Water
Some prefer to add the strained contents of a pot of tea. Stir well and decorate with fruits in season. Serve in 4 oz. punch glasses.

Champagne Velvet

See Black Velvet on page 9.

Champs Élysées Cocktail

1 oz. Cognac
½ oz. Yellow Chartreuse
Juice of ¼ Lemon
½ Teaspoon Powdered Sugar
1 Dash Bitters
Shake well with cracked ice and strain into 3 oz. cocktail glass. Old Mr. Boston Five Star Brandy may be substituted for Cognac.

Charles Cocktail

1¼ oz. Sweet Vermouth
1¼ oz. Old Mr. Boston Five Star Brandy
1 Dash Bitters
Stir well with cracked ice and strain into 3 oz. cocktail glass.

C

Chelsea Side Car Cocktail

Juice of ¼ Lemon
¾ oz. Triple Sec
¾ oz. Old Mr. Boston Dry Gin
Shake well with cracked ice and strain into 3 oz. cocktail glass.

Cherry Blossom Cocktail

1 oz. Old Mr. Boston Wild Cherry Flavored Brandy
1 oz. Old Mr. Boston Five Star Brandy
¼ Teaspoon Curacao
¼ Teaspoon Lemon Juice
¼ Teaspoon Grenadine
Shake well with cracked ice and strain into 3 oz. cocktail glass.

Cherry Fizz

Juice ½ Lemon
2 oz. Old Mr. Boston Wild Cherry Flavored Brandy
Shake well with cracked ice and strain into 7 oz. highball glass. Fill with carbonated water and decorate with a cherry.

Cherry Flip

1 Egg
1 Teaspoon Powdered Sugar
1½ oz. Old Mr. Boston Wild Cherry Flavored Brandy
2 Teaspoons Sweet Cream (if desired)
Shake well with cracked ice and strain into 5 oz. flip glass. Grate a little nutmeg on top.

Cherry Sling

2 Cubes of Ice
2 oz. Old Mr. Boston Wild Cherry Flavored Brandy
Juice ½ Lemon
Serve in Old Fashioned cocktail glass and stir. Twist of lemon peel and drop in glass.

Chicago Cocktail

2 oz. Old Mr. Boston Five Star Brandy
1 Dash Bitters
¼ Teaspoon Curacao
Stir well with cracked ice and strain into 3 oz. cocktail glass. Frost glass by rubbing slice of lemon around rim and then dip in powdered sugar.

Chicago Fizz

Juice ½ Lemon
1 Teaspoon Powdered Sugar
White of 1 Egg
1 oz. Port Wine
1 oz. Old Mr. Boston Imported Rum
Shake well with cracked ice and strain into 7 oz. highball glass. Fill with carbonated water and stir.

Chinese Cocktail

½ oz. Grenadine
1½ oz. Jamaica Rum
1 Dash Bitters
1 Teaspoon Maraschino
1 Teaspoon Curacao
Shake well with cracked ice and strain into 3 oz. cocktail glass.

C

Chocolate Cocktail

1½ oz. Port Wine
¼ oz. Yellow Chartreuse
Yolk of 1 Egg
1 Teaspoon Powdered Sugar
Shake well with cracked ice and strain into 4 oz. cocktail glass.

Chocolate Daisy

Juice ½ Lemon
½ Teaspoon Powdered Sugar
1 Teaspoon Raspberry Syrup or Grenadine
1½ oz. Old Mr. Boston Five Star Brandy
1½ oz. Port Wine
Shake well with cracked ice and strain into stein or 8 oz. metal cup. Add cube of ice and decorate with fruit.

Chocolate Flip

1 Egg
1 Teaspoon of Powdered Sugar
¾ oz. Old Mr. Boston Sloe Gin
¾ oz. Old Mr. Boston Five Star Brandy
2 Teaspoons Sweet Cream (if desired)
Shake well with cracked ice and strain into 5 oz. flip glass. Grate a little nutmeg on top.

Chocolate Soldier Cocktail

Juice ½ Lime
¾ oz. Dubonnet
1½ oz. Old Mr. Boston Dry Gin
Shake well with cracked ice and strain into 3 oz. cocktail glass.

Christmas Yule Eggnog

Beat the yolks and whites of 1 Dozen Eggs separately and then pour together and add:
1 Pinch Baking Soda
6 oz. Old Mr. Boston Imported Rum
2 lbs. Granulated Sugar
Beat into stiff batter. Then add:
1 qt. Milk
1 qt. Sweet Cream
2 qts. Old Mr. Boston Whiskey*
Stir. Set in refrigerator over night. Before serving, stir again, and serve in 4 oz. punch glasses, and grate nutmeg on top.

Cider Cup

Use Large Glass Pitcher
4 Teaspoons Powdered Sugar
6 oz. Carbonated Water
½ oz. Triple Sec
½ oz. Curacao
2 oz. Old Mr. Boston Five Star Brandy
Fill pitcher with cubes of ice. Add 1 pint of cider. Stir well and decorate with as many fruits as available and also rind of cucumber inserted on each side of pitcher. Top with small bunch of mint sprigs. Serve in 5 oz. claret glasses.

Cider Eggnog

1 Egg
1 Teaspoon Powdered Sugar
¼ pt. Milk
Shake well with cracked ice and strain into 12 oz. Tom Collins glass. Then fill glass with sweet cider and stir. Grate nutmeg on top.

* *Bourbon, Blended, Rye or Canadian*

C

Clam and Tomato Cocktail

1½ oz. Old Mr. Boston Vodka
1 oz. Clam Juice
3 oz. Tomato Juice
Shake well with cracked ice, strain, and serve on the rocks in large Old Fashioned glass.

Claret Cobbler

Dissolve: 1 teaspoon powdered sugar in 2 oz. carbonated water; then add 3 oz. Claret. Fill 10 oz. goblet with shaved ice and stir. Decorate with fruits in season. Serve with straws.

Claret Cup

Use Large Glass Pitcher
4 Teaspoons Powdered Sugar
6 oz. Carbonated Water
½ oz. Triple Sec
½ oz. Curacao
2 oz. Old Mr. Boston Five Star Brandy
Fill pitcher with cubes of ice. Add 1 pint of Claret. Stir well and decorate with as many fruits as available and also rind of cucumber inserted on each side of pitcher. Top with small bunch of mint sprigs. Serve in 5 oz. claret glass.

Claret Punch

Juice of 1 Dozen Lemons
Add enough powdered sugar to sweeten. Place large block of ice in punch bowl and stir well. Then add:
½ pt. Curacao
1 pt. Old Mr. Boston Five Star Brandy
3 qts. Claret
1 qt. Carbonated Water
Some prefer to add the strained contents of a pot of tea. Stir well and decorate with fruits in season. Serve in 4 oz. punch glasses.

Claridge Cocktail

¾ oz. Old Mr. Boston Dry Gin
¾ oz. Dry Vermouth
½ oz. Old Mr. Boston Apricot Flavored Brandy
½ oz. Triple Sec
Stir well with cracked ice and strain into 3 oz. cocktail glass.

Classic Cocktail

Juice of ¼ Lemon
¼ oz. Curacao
¼ oz. Maraschino
1 oz. Old Mr. Boston Five Star Brandy
Shake well with cracked ice and strain into 3 oz. cocktail glass. Frost rim of glass by rubbing with lemon and dipping in powdered sugar.

Clove Cocktail

1 oz. Sweet Vermouth
½ oz. Old Mr. Boston Sloe Gin
½ oz. Muscatel Wine
Stir well with cracked ice and strain into 3 oz. cocktail glass.

C

Clover Club Cocktail

Juice ½ Lemon
2 Teaspoons Grenadine
White of 1 Egg
1½ oz. Old Mr. Boston Dry Gin
Shake well with cracked ice and strain into 4 oz. cocktail glass.

Clover Leaf Cocktail

Juice 1 Lime
2 Teaspoons Grenadine
White of 1 Egg
1½ oz. Old Mr. Boston Dry Gin
Shake well with cracked ice and strain into 4 oz. cocktail glass. Serve with mint leaf on top.

Club Cocktail

1½ oz. Old Mr. Boston Dry Gin
¾ oz. Sweet Vermouth
Stir well with cracked ice and strain into 3 oz. cocktail glass. Add a cherry or olive.

Cobblers

See Index on page 139 for complete list of Cobbler *recipes.*

Coffee Cocktail

1 Egg
1 Teaspoon Powdered Sugar
1 oz. Port Wine
1 oz. Old Mr. Boston Five Star Brandy
Shake well with cracked ice and strain into 5 oz. cocktail glass. Grate nutmeg on top.

Coffee Flip

1 Egg
1 Teaspoon Powdered Sugar
1 oz. Old Mr. Boston Five Star Brandy
1 oz. Port Wine
2 Teaspoons Sweet Cream (if desired)
Shake well with cracked ice and strain into 5 oz. flip glass. Grate a little nutmeg on top.

Cognac Highball

1 Cube of Ice
2 oz. Cognac
Fill 8 oz. highball glass with ginger ale or carbonated water. Add twist of lemon peel, if desired, and stir gently.

Cold Deck Cocktail

½ oz. Old Mr. Boston Creme de Menthe (White)
½ oz. Sweet Vermouth
1 oz. Old Mr. Boston Five Star Brandy
Stir well with cracked ice and strain into 3 oz. cocktail glass.

Collins

See Index on page 139 for complete list of Collins *recipes.*

Colonial Cocktail

½ oz. Grapefruit Juice
1 Teaspoon Maraschino
1½ oz. Old Mr. Boston Dry Gin
Shake well with cracked ice and strain into 3 oz. cocktail glass. Serve with an olive.

TWIST TO OPEN
IMPORTED
Old Mr. Boston
IMPORTED
Canadian
RIVER
WHISKY · A BLEND
86.8 PROOF
IMPORTED
Old Mr. Boston
Canadian
WHISKY
A BLEND
This fine Imported Canadian Whisky has been carefully selected to give you the delightfully smooth and mellow quality that has made Canadian Whiskies so famous
DISTILLED, AGED AND BLENDED UNDER THE SUPERVISION OF THE CANADIAN GOVERNMENT
Eighty Proof - just like in Canada
FOUR-FIFTHS QUART
IMPORTED AND BOTTLED BY MR. BOSTON DISTILLER INC. BOSTON, MASSACHUSETTS.

C

Commodore Cocktail

Juice ½ Lime or ¼ Lemon
1 Teaspoon Powdered Sugar
2 Dashes Orange Bitters
1½ oz. Old Mr. Boston Whiskey*
Shake well with cracked ice and strain into 3 oz. cocktail glass.

Coolers

See Index on page 140 for complete list of Cooler *recipes.*

Cooperstown Cocktail

½ oz. Dry Vermouth
½ oz. Sweet Vermouth
1 oz. Old Mr. Boston Dry Gin
2 Sprigs Fresh Mint
Shake well with cracked ice and strain into 3 oz. cocktail glass.

Cornell Cocktail

½ Teaspoon Lemon Juice
1 Teaspoon Maraschino
White of 1 Egg
1½ oz. Old Mr. Boston Dry Gin
Shake well with cracked ice and strain into 4 oz. cocktail glass.

Coronation Cocktail

¾ oz. Old Mr. Boston Dry Gin
¾ oz. Dubonnet
¾ oz. Dry Vermouth
Stir well with cracked ice and strain into 3 oz. cocktail glass.

Country Club Cooler

Into 12 oz. Tom Collins glass, put:
½ Teaspoon Grenadine
2 oz. Carbonated Water *and stir.*
Fill glass with cracked ice and add:
2 oz. Dry Vermouth
Fill with carbonated water or ginger ale and stir again. Insert spiral of orange or lemon peel (or both) and dangle end over rim of glass.

Cowboy Cocktail

1½ oz. Old Mr. Boston Whiskey*
½ oz. Sweet Cream
Shake well with cracked ice and strain into 3 oz. cocktail glass.

Cream Fizz

Juice ½ Lemon
1 Teaspoon Powdered Sugar
2 oz. Old Mr. Boston Dry Gin
1 Teaspoon Fresh Cream
Shake well with cracked ice and strain into 8 oz. highball glass. Fill with carbonated water and stir.

Cream Puff

2 oz. Old Mr. Boston Imported Rum
1 oz. Sweet Cream
½ Teaspoon Powdered Sugar
Shake well with cracked ice and strain into 8 oz. highball glass. Fill with carbonated water and stir.

* Bourbon, Blended, Rye or Canadian.

C

CREME DE GIN COCKTAIL

1½ oz. Old Mr. Boston Dry Gin
½ oz. Old Mr. Boston Creme de Menthe (white)
White of 1 Egg
2 Teaspoons Lemon Juice
2 Teaspoons Orange Juice
Shake well with cracked ice and strain into 4 oz. cocktail glass.

CREME DE MENTHE FRAPPE

Fill cocktail glass up to brim with shaved ice. Add Old Mr. Boston Creme de Menthe (green). Serve with two short straws.

CREOLE LADY COCKTAIL

1¼ oz. Old Mr. Boston Whiskey*
1¼ oz. Madeira Wine
1 Teaspoon Grenadine
Stir well with cracked ice and strain into 3 oz. cocktail glass. Serve with 1 green and 1 red cherry.

CRIMSON COCKTAIL

1½ oz. Old Mr. Boston Dry Gin
2 Teaspoons Lemon Juice
1 Teaspoon Grenadine
Shake well with cracked ice and strain into 3 oz. cocktail glass, leaving enough room on top to float ¾ oz. Port Wine.

CRYSTAL SLIPPER COCKTAIL

½ oz. Creme de Yvette
2 Dashes Orange Bitters
1½ oz. Old Mr. Boston Dry Gin
Stir well with cracked ice and strain into 3 oz. cocktail glass.

CUBA LIBRE

Juice ½ Lime
Drop rind in glass.
2 oz. Old Mr. Boston Imported Rum
2 Cubes of Ice
Fill glass with any cola. Use 10 oz. glass and stir well.

CUBAN COCKTAIL NO. 1

Juice of ½ Lime
½ Teaspoon Powdered Sugar
2 oz. Old Mr. Boston Imported Rum
Shake well with cracked ice and strain into 3 oz. cocktail glass.

CUBAN COCKTAIL NO. 2

Juice of ½ Lime or ¼ Lemon
½ oz. Old Mr. Boston Apricot Flavored Brandy
1½ oz. Old Mr. Boston Five Star Brandy
1 Teaspoon Old Mr. Boston Imported Rum
Shake well with cracked ice and strain into 3 oz. cocktail glass.

CUBAN SPECIAL COCKTAIL

½ oz. Pineapple Juice
Juice ½ Lime
1 oz. Old Mr. Boston Imported Rum
½ Teaspoon Curacao
Shake well with cracked ice and strain into 3 oz. cocktail glass. Decorate with stick of pineapple and a cherry.

CUPS

See Index on page 140 for complete list of CUP *recipes.*

* *Bourbon, Blended, Rye or Canadian.*

Daiquiri Cocktail

Juice 1 Lime
1 Teaspoon Powdered Sugar
1½ oz. Old Mr. Boston Imported Rum
Shake well with cracked ice and strain into 3 oz. cocktail glass.

Daisies

See Index on page 141 for complete list of Daisy *recipes.*

Damn-the-Weather Cocktail

1 Teaspoon Curacao
½ oz. Orange Juice
½ oz. Sweet Vermouth
1 oz. Old Mr. Boston Dry Gin
Shake well with cracked ice and strain into 3 oz. cocktail glass.

Darb Cocktail

1 Teaspoon Lemon Juice
¾ oz. Dry Vermouth
¾ oz. Old Mr. Boston Dry Gin
¾ oz. Old Mr. Boston Apricot Flavored Brandy
Shake well with cracked ice and strain into 3 oz. cocktail glass.

Deauville Cocktail

Juice of ¼ Lemon
½ oz. Old Mr. Boston Five Star Brandy
½ oz. Apple Brandy
½ oz. Triple Sec
Shake well with cracked ice and strain into 3 oz. cocktail glass.

Deep Sea Cocktail

1 oz. Dry Vermouth
¼ Teaspoon Absinthe Substitute
1 Dash Orange Bitters
1 oz. Old Mr. Boston Dry Gin
Stir well with cracked ice and strain into 3 oz. cocktail glass.

Dempsey Cocktail

1 oz. Old Mr. Boston Dry Gin
1 oz. Apple Brandy
½ Teaspoon Absinthe Substitute
½ Teaspoon Grenadine
Stir well with cracked ice and strain into 3 oz. cocktail glass.

D

Derby Fizz
Juice ½ Lemon
1 Teaspoon Powdered Sugar
1 Egg
2 oz. Old Mr. Boston Scotch Whisky
1 Teaspoon Curacao
Shake well with cracked ice and strain into 8 oz. highball glass. Fill with carbonated water and stir.

Devil's Cocktail
½ Teaspoon Lemon Juice
1¼ oz. Port Wine
1¼ oz. Dry Vermouth
Stir well with cracked ice and strain into 3 oz. cocktail glass.

Diamond Fizz
Juice ½ Lemon
1 Teaspoon Powdered Sugar
2 oz. Old Mr. Boston Dry Gin
Shake well with cracked ice and strain into 7 oz. highball glass. Fill with champagne and stir gently.

Diana Cocktail
Fill 3 oz. cocktail glass with shaved ice, then fill ¾ full with Old Mr. Boston Creme de Menthe (white) *and float* Old Mr. Boston Five Star Brandy *on top.*

Dillatini Cocktail
See *Special Martini Section* on pages 116 and 117.

Dinah Cocktail
Juice of ¼ Lemon
½ Teaspoon Powdered Sugar
1½ oz. Old Mr. Boston Whiskey*
2 or 3 Sprigs Fresh Mint
Shake very well with cracked ice and strain into 3 oz. cocktail glass. Serve with a mint leaf.

Diplomat Cocktail
1½ oz. Dry Vermouth
½ oz. Sweet Vermouth
2 Dashes Bitters
½ Teaspoon Maraschino
Stir well with cracked ice and strain into 3 oz. cocktail glass. Serve with ½ slice of lemon and a cherry.

Dixie Cocktail
Juice of ¼ Orange
½ oz. Absinthe Substitute
½ oz. Dry Vermouth
1 oz. Old Mr. Boston Dry Gin
Shake well with cracked ice and strain into 4 oz. cocktail glass.

Dixie Julep
Into a 12 oz. Tom Collins glass put
4 Sprigs of Mint
1 Teaspoon Powdered Sugar
2½ oz. Old Mr. Boston Kentucky Bourbon Whiskey
Fill with shaved ice and stir gently until glass is frosted. Decorate with sprigs of mint. Serve with straws.

Dixie Whiskey Cocktail
½ Lump of Sugar
1 Dash Bitters
¼ Teaspoon Curacao
½ Teaspoon Old Mr. Boston Creme de Menthe (white)
2 oz. Old Mr. Boston Whiskey*
Shake well with cracked ice and strain into 3 oz. cocktail glass.

---

* *Bourbon, Blended, Rye or Canadian.*

D

Double Standard Sour

Juice ½ Lemon or 1 Lime
½ Teaspoon Powdered Sugar
¾ oz. Old Mr. Boston Whiskey*
¾ oz. Old Mr. Boston Dry Gin
½ Teaspoon Raspberry Syrup or Grenadine
Shake well with cracked ice and strain into 6 oz. sour glass. Decorate with a half-slice of lemon and a cherry.

Dream Cocktail

¾ oz. Curacao
1½ oz. Old Mr. Boston Five Star Brandy
¼ Teaspoon Old Mr. Boston Anisette
Shake well with cracked ice and strain into 3 oz. cocktail glass.

Dry Martini Cocktail

See *Special Martini Section* on pages 116 and 117.

Du Barry Cocktail

1 Dash Bitters
¾ oz. Dry Vermouth
½ Teaspoon Absinthe Substitute
1½ oz. Old Mr. Boston Dry Gin
Stir well with cracked ice and strain into 3 oz. cocktail glass. Add slice of orange.

Dubonnet Cocktail

1½ oz. Dubonnet
¾ oz. Old Mr. Boston Dry Gin
1 Dash Orange Bitters *if desired.*
Stir well with cracked ice and strain into 3 oz. cocktail glass. Twist of lemon peel on top and drop in glass.

Dubonnet Fizz

Juice ½ Orange
Juice ¼ Lemon
1 Teaspoon Old Mr. Boston Wild Cherry Flavored Brandy
2 oz. Dubonnet
Shake well with cracked ice and strain into 7 oz. highball glass. Fill with carbonated water and stir.

Dubonnet Highball

1 Cube of Ice
2 oz. Dubonnet
Fill 8 oz. highball glass with ginger ale or carbonated water. Add twist of lemon peel, if desired, and stir.

Duchess Cocktail

¾ oz. Dry Vermouth
¾ oz. Sweet Vermouth
¾ oz. Absinthe Substitute
Stir well with cracked ice and strain into 3 oz. cocktail glass.

Duke Cocktail

½ oz. Triple Sec
1 Teaspoon Orange Juice
2 Teaspoons Lemon Juice
½ Teaspoon Maraschino
1 Egg
Shake well with cracked ice and strain into 8 oz. stem glass. Fill with Champagne and stir very gently.

* *Bourbon, Blended, Rye or Canadian.*

East India Cocktail No. 1

1½ oz. Old Mr. Boston Five Star Brandy
½ Teaspoon Pineapple Juice
½ Teaspoon Curacao
1 Teaspoon Jamaica Rum
1 Dash Bitters
Shake well with cracked ice and strain into 3 oz. cocktail glass. Twist of lemon peel and add a cherry.

East India Cocktail No. 2

1¼ oz. Dry Vermouth
1¼ oz. Sherry Wine
1 Dash Orange Bitters
Stir well with cracked ice and strain into 3 oz. cocktail glass.

Eclipse Cocktail

1 oz. Old Mr. Boston Dry Gin
2 oz. Old Mr. Boston Sloe Gin
½ Teaspoon Lemon Juice
Put enough grenadine into 4 oz. cocktail glass to cover a ripe olive. Mix the above ingredients in ice and pour gently onto the grenadine so that they do not mix.

Eggnogs

See *Special Eggnog Section* on pages 114 and 115 and also Index on page 143 for complete list of Eggnog recipes.

Egg Sour

1 Egg
1 Teaspoon Powdered Sugar
Juice ½ Lemon
2 oz. Old Mr. Boston Five Star Brandy
¼ Teaspoon Curacao
Shake well with cracked ice and strain into 8 oz. highball glass.

El Presidente Cocktail No. 1

Juice 1 Lime
1 Teaspoon Pineapple Juice
1 Teaspoon Grenadine
1½ oz. Old Mr. Boston Imported Rum
Shake well with cracked ice and strain into 3 oz. cocktail glass.

El Presidente Cocktail No. 2

¾ oz. Dry Vermouth
1½ oz. Old Mr. Boston Imported Rum
1 Dash Bitters
Stir well with cracked ice and strain into 3 oz. cocktail glass.

E

Elk's Own Cocktail
White of 1 Egg
1½ oz. Old Mr. Boston Whiskey*
¾ oz. Port Wine
Juice ¼ Lemon
1 Teaspoon Powdered Sugar
Add a strip of Pineapple. Shake well with cracked ice and strain into 4 oz. cocktail glass.

Emerald Isle Cocktail
2 oz. Old Mr. Boston Dry Gin
1 Teaspoon Old Mr. Boston
   Creme de Menthe (Green)
3 Dashes Bitters
Stir well with cracked ice and strain into 3 oz. cocktail glass.

English Highball
1 Cube of Ice
¾ oz. Old Mr. Boston Dry Gin
¾ oz. Old Mr. Boston Five Star Brandy
¾ oz. Sweet Vermouth
Fill 8 oz. highball glass with ginger ale or carbonated water. Add twist of lemon peel, if desired, and stir.

English Rose Cocktail
1¼ oz. Old Mr. Boston Dry Gin
¾ oz. Old Mr. Boston Apricot
   Flavored Brandy
¾ oz. Dry Vermouth
1 Teaspoon Grenadine
¼ Teaspoon Lemon Juice
Shake well with cracked ice and strain into 4 oz. cocktail glass. Frost rim of glass by rubbing with lemon and dipping in sugar. Serve with a cherry.

Ethel Duffy Cocktail
¾ oz. Old Mr. Boston Apricot
   Flavored Brandy
¾ oz. Old Mr. Boston Creme de
   Menthe (White)
¾ oz. Curacao
Shake well with cracked ice and strain into 3 oz. cocktail glass.

Everybody's Irish Cocktail
1 Teaspoon Old Mr. Boston
   Creme de Menthe (Green)
1 Teaspoon Green Chartreuse
2 oz. Irish Whiskey
Stir well with cracked ice and strain into 3 oz. cocktail glass. Serve with green olive.

Eye-opener Cocktail
Yolk of 1 Egg
½ Teaspoon Powdered Sugar
1 Teaspoon Absinthe Substitute
1 Teaspoon Curacao
1 Teaspoon Old Mr. Boston
   Creme de Cacao
2 oz. Old Mr. Boston Imported Rum
Shake well with cracked ice and strain into 4 oz. cocktail glass.

* *Bourbon, Blended, Rye or Canadian.*

Old Mr. Boston Scotch Whisky 80 and 86 Proof Imported From Scotland ▶

FROM
SCOTLAND
IMPORTED FROM SCOTLAND
Old Mr. Boston
PRODUCT OF SCOTLAND
BLENDED
SCOTCH
WHISKY
100% SCOTCH WHISKIES
THIS IS TRULY THE MILDEST SCOTCH WHISKY
MADE FROM CHOICE HIGHLAND STOCKS
EIGHTY SIX PROOF • FOUR-FIFTHS QUART
DISTILLED AND BLENDED IN SCOTLAND • IMPORTED AND BOTTLED BY
MR. BOSTON DISTILLER INC., BOSTON, MASSACHUSETTS
Eighty Six Proof
IMPORTED

Fair and Warmer Cocktail

¾ oz. Sweet Vermouth
1½ oz. Old Mr. Boston Imported Rum
½ Teaspoon Curacao
Stir well with cracked ice and strain into 3 oz. cocktail glass.

Fairy Belle Cocktail

White of 1 Egg
1 Teaspoon Grenadine
¾ oz. Old Mr. Boston Apricot Flavored Brandy
1½ oz. Old Mr. Boston Dry Gin
Shake well with cracked ice and strain into 4 oz. cocktail glass.

Fallen Angel Cocktail

Juice of 1 Lemon or ½ Lime
1½ oz. Old Mr. Boston Dry Gin
1 Dash Bitters
½ Teaspoon Old Mr. Boston Creme de Menthe (white)
Shake well with cracked ice and strain into 3 oz. cocktail glass. Serve with a cherry.

Fancy Brandy Cocktail

2 oz. Old Mr. Boston Five Star Brandy
1 Dash Bitters
¼ Teaspoon Curacao
¼ Teaspoon Powdered Sugar
Shake well with cracked ice and strain into 3 oz. cocktail glass. Twist of lemon peel and drop in glass.

Fancy Gin Cocktail

Same as Fancy Brandy Cocktail *except substitute:* 2 oz. Old Mr. Boston Dry Gin

Fancy Whiskey Cocktail

Same as Fancy Brandy Cocktail *except substitute:* 2 oz. Old Mr. Boston Whiskey*

Fantasio Cocktail

1 Teaspoon Old Mr. Boston Creme de Menthe (White)
1 Teaspoon Maraschino
1 oz. Old Mr. Boston Five Star Brandy
¾ oz. Dry Vermouth
Stir well with cracked ice and strain into 3 oz. cocktail glass.

* Bourbon, Blended, Rye or Canadian.

F

Farmer's Cocktail

1 oz. Old Mr. Boston Dry Gin
½ oz. Dry Vermouth
½ oz. Sweet Vermouth
2 Dashes Bitters
Stir well with cracked ice and strain into 3 oz. cocktail glass.

Favourite Cocktail

¾ oz. Old Mr. Boston Apricot Flavored Brandy
¾ oz. Dry Vermouth
¾ oz. Old Mr. Boston Dry Gin
¼ Teaspoon Lemon Juice
Shake well with cracked ice and strain into 3 oz. cocktail glass.

Fifth Avenue

⅓ oz. Old Mr. Boston Creme de Cacao
⅓ oz. Old Mr. Boston Apricot Flavored Brandy
⅓ oz. Sweet Cream
Pour carefully, in order given, into Pousse Café glass, so that each ingredient floats on preceding one.

Fifty-Fifty Cocktail

1¼ oz. Old Mr. Boston Dry Gin
1¼ oz. Dry Vermouth
Stir well with cracked ice and strain into 3 oz. cocktail glass.

Fine and Dandy Cocktail

Juice of ¼ Lemon
½ oz. Triple Sec
1¼ oz. Old Mr. Boston Dry Gin
1 Dash Bitters
Shake well with cracked ice and strain into 3 oz. cocktail glass. Serve with a cherry.

Fireman's Sour

Juice 2 Limes
½ Teaspoon Powdered Sugar
½ oz. Grenadine
2 oz. Old Mr. Boston Imported Rum
Shake well with cracked ice and strain into Delmonico glass. Fill with carbonated water, if desired. Decorate with a half-slice of lemon and a cherry.

Fish House Punch

Juice of 1 Dozen Lemons
Add enough Powdered Sugar to sweeten. Place large block of ice in punch bowl and stir well. Then add:
1½ qts. Old Mr. Boston Five Star Brandy
1 pt. Old Mr. Boston Peach Flavored Brandy
1 pt. Old Mr. Boston Imported Rum
1 qt. Carbonated Water
Some prefer to add the strained contents of a pot of tea. Stir well and decorate with fruits in season. Serve in 4 oz. Punch glasses.

Fixes

See Index on page 143 for complete list of Fix *recipes.*

Fizzes

See Index on page 143 for complete list of Fizz *recipes.*

37

F

Flamingo Cocktail
Juice of ½ Lime
½ oz. Old Mr. Boston Apricot Flavored Brandy
1¼ oz. Old Mr. Boston Dry Gin
1 Teaspoon Grenadine
Shake well with cracked ice and strain into 3 oz. cocktail glass.

Flips
See Index on page 143 for complete list of Flip *recipes.*

Floradora Cooler
Into 12 oz. Tom Collins glass, put:
Juice 1 Lime
½ Teaspoon Powdered Sugar
½ oz. Raspberry Syrup or Grenadine
2 oz. Carbonated Water, *and stir*
Fill glass with cracked ice and add:
2 oz. Old Mr. Boston Dry Gin. *Fill with carbonated water or ginger ale and stir again.*

Flying Grasshopper Cocktail
¾ oz. Old Mr. Boston Creme de Menthe (green)
¾ oz. Old Mr. Boston Creme de Cacao (white)
¾ oz. Old Mr. Boston Vodka
Stir well with cracked ice and strain into 3 oz. cocktail glass.

Flying Scotchman Cocktail
1 oz. Sweet Vermouth
1 oz. Old Mr. Boston Scotch Whisky
1 Dash Bitters
¼ Teaspoon Simple Syrup
Stir well with cracked ice and strain into 3 oz. cocktail glass.

Fog Horn
1 Cube of Ice
Juice of ½ Lime
1½ oz. Old Mr. Boston Dry Gin
Fill 8 oz. highball glass with ginger ale and stir. Leave lime in glass.

Fox River Cocktail
½ oz. Old Mr. Boston Creme de Cacao
2 oz. Old Mr. Boston Whiskey*
4 Dashes Bitters
Stir well with cracked ice and strain into 3 oz. cocktail glass.

Frankenjack Cocktail
1 oz. Old Mr. Boston Dry Gin
¾ oz. Dry Vermouth
½ oz. Old Mr. Boston Apricot Flavored Brandy
1 Teaspoon Triple Sec
Stir well with cracked ice and strain into 3 oz. cocktail glass. Serve with a cherry.

French "75"
Juice of 1 Lemon
2 Teaspoons Powdered Sugar
Stir well in 12 oz. Tom Collins glass. Then add 1 Cube of Ice, 2 oz. Old Mr. Boston Dry Gin and fill with Champagne and stir gently. Decorate with slice of lemon, orange and a cherry. Serve with straws.

* *Bourbon, Blended, Rye or Canadian.*

G

Frisco Sour
Juice ¼ Lemon
Juice ½ Lime
½ oz. Benedictine
2 oz. Old Mr. Boston Whiskey*
Shake well with cracked ice and strain into 6 oz. sour glass. Decorate with slices of lemon and lime.

Froth Blower Cocktail
White of 1 Egg
1 Teaspoon Grenadine
2 oz. Old Mr. Boston Dry Gin
Shake well with cracked ice and strain into 4 oz. cocktail glass.

Froupe Cocktail
1¼ oz. Sweet Vermouth
1¼ oz. Old Mr. Boston Five Star Brandy
1 Teaspoon Benedictine
Stir well with cracked ice and strain into 3 oz. cocktail glass.

Frozen Daiquiri Cocktail
Juice 1 Lime
1 Teaspoon Powdered Sugar
2 oz. Old Mr. Boston Imported Rum
Agitate in electric mixer filled with shaved ice for about 2 minutes. Strain through coarse meshed strainer into 6 oz. Champagne glass.

General Harrison's Eggnog
1 Egg
1 Teaspoon Powdered Sugar
Shake well with cracked ice and strain into 12 oz. Tom Collins glass. Fill glass with Claret or sweet cider and stir gently. Grate nutmeg on top.

Gibson Cocktail
See *Special Martini Section* on pages 116 and 117.

Gilroy Cocktail
Juice of ¼ Lemon
½ oz. Dry Vermouth
¾ oz. Old Mr. Boston Wild Cherry Flavored Brandy
¾ oz. Old Mr. Boston Dry Gin
1 Dash Orange Bitters
Shake well with cracked ice and strain into 3 oz. cocktail glass.

* *Bourbon, Blended, Rye or Canadian.*

G

Gimlet Cocktail
Juice 1 Lime
1 Teaspoon Powdered Sugar
1½ oz. Old Mr. Boston Dry Gin
Shake well with cracked ice and strain into 4 oz. cocktail glass.

Gin and Bitters
Put ½ teaspoon bitters into 3 oz. cocktail glass and revolve glass until it is entirely coated with the bitters. Then fill with Old Mr. Boston Dry Gin. *No ice is used in this drink.*

Gin and It (English)
2 oz. Old Mr. Boston Dry Gin
1 oz. Sweet Vermouth
Stir. No ice is used in this drink. Serve in 3 oz. cocktail glass.

Gin and Tonic
2 oz. Old Mr. Boston Dry Gin
Cube of Ice
Fill glass with quinine water and stir. Use 12 oz. Tom Collins glass.

Gin Buck
1 Cube of Ice
Juice of ½ Lemon
1½ oz. Old Mr. Boston Dry Gin
Fill 8 oz. highball glass with ginger ale and stir.

Gin Cobbler
Dissolve: 1 Teaspoon Powdered Sugar *in* 2 oz. Carbonated Water, *then fill* 10 oz. goblet *with shaved ice, and add*
2 oz. Old Mr. Boston Dry Gin
Stir well and decorate with fruits in season. Serve with straws.

Gin Cocktail
2 oz. Old Mr. Boston Dry Gin
2 Dashes Bitters
Stir well with cracked ice and strain into 3 oz. cocktail glass. Serve with a twist of lemon peel.

Gin Cooler
Into 12 oz. Tom Collins glass, put:
½ Teaspoon Powdered Sugar
2 oz. Carbonated Water, *and stir*
Fill glass with cracked ice and add:
2 oz. Old Mr. Boston Dry Gin
Fill with carbonated water or ginger ale and stir again. Insert spiral of orange or lemon peel (or both) and dangle end over rim of glass.

Gin Daisy
Juice of ½ Lemon
½ Teaspoon Powdered Sugar
1 Teaspoon Raspberry Syrup or Grenadine
2 oz. Old Mr. Boston Dry Gin
Shake well with cracked ice and strain into stein or 8 oz. metal cup. Add cube of ice and decorate with fruit.

Gin Fix
Juice ½ Lemon
1 Teaspoon Powdered Sugar
1 Teaspoon Water
Stir and fill glass with shaved ice. Add
2½ oz. Old Mr. Boston Dry Gin
Use 8 oz. highball glass. Stir well. Add slice of lemon. Serve with straws.

G

Gin Fizz

Juice ½ Lemon
1 Teaspoon Powdered Sugar
2 oz. Old Mr. Boston Dry Gin
Shake well with cracked ice and strain into 7 oz. highball glass. Fill with carbonated water and stir.

Gin Highball

1 Cube of Ice
2 oz. Old Mr. Boston Dry Gin
Fill 8 oz. highball glass with ginger ale or carbonated water. Add twist of lemon peel, if desired, and stir.

Gin Milk Punch

1 Teaspoon Powdered Sugar
2 oz. Old Mr. Boston Dry Gin
½ pt. Milk
Shake well with cracked ice, strain into 12 oz. Tom Collins glass and grate nutmeg on top.

Gin Rickey

1 Cube of Ice
Juice ½ Lime
1½ oz. Old Mr. Boston Dry Gin
Fill 8 oz. highball glass with carbonated water and stir. Leave lime in glass.

Gin Sangaree

Dissolve ½ teaspoon powdered sugar in 1 teaspoon of water. Add
2 oz. Old Mr. Boston Dry Gin
2 cubes of ice.
Serve in 8 oz. highball glass. Fill balance with soda water. Stir, leaving enough room on which to float a tablespoon of Port Wine. Sprinkle lightly with nutmeg.

Gin Sling

Dissolve 1 teaspoon powdered sugar in 1 teaspoon water and juice ½ lemon.
2 oz. Old Mr. Boston Dry Gin
2 Cubes of Ice
Serve in Old Fashioned cocktail glass and stir. Twist of orange peel and drop in glass.

Gin Smash

Muddle 1 Lump of Sugar with
1 oz. Carbonated Water and
4 Sprigs of Green Mint
Add 2 oz. Old Mr. Boston Dry Gin and a cube of ice. Stir and decorate with a slice of orange and a cherry. Twist lemon peel on top. Use Old Fashioned cocktail glass.

Gin Sour

Juice of ½ Lemon
½ Teaspoon Powdered Sugar
2 oz. Old Mr. Boston Dry Gin
Shake well with cracked ice and strain into 6 oz. sour glass. Decorate with a half-slice of lemon and a cherry.

OLD
Mr. BOSTON
Fine Liquors
GENUINE
IMPORTED
RUM
IMPORTED
OLD
Mr. BOSTON
BRAND
RUM
RUM IS IMPORTED FROM THE VIRGIN ISLANDS
IN THE WEST INDIES
BOTTLED BY MR. BOSTON DISTILLER INC. BOSTON, MASS.

G

Gin Squirt
1½ oz. Old Mr. Boston Dry Gin
1 Tablespoon Powdered Sugar
1 Teaspoon Raspberry Syrup or Grenadine
Stir well with cracked ice and strain into 8 oz. highball glass; fill with carbonated water and stir. Decorate with cubes of pineapple and strawberries.

Gin Swizzle
Into 12 oz. Tom Collins glass put:
Juice 1 Lime
1 Teaspoon Powdered Sugar
2 oz. Carbonated Water
Fill glass with shaved ice and stir thoroughly with swizzle stick. Then add:
2 Dashes Bitters
2 oz. Old Mr. Boston Dry Gin
Fill with carbonated water and serve with swizzle stick in glass, allowing individual to do final stirring.

Gin Toddy
Use Old Fashioned cocktail glass.
½ Teaspoon Powdered Sugar
2 Teaspoons Water *and stir.*
2 oz. Old Mr. Boston Dry Gin
1 Lump of Ice
Stir well and twist lemon peel on top.

Gin Toddy (Hot)
Put lump of sugar into hot whiskey glass and fill two-thirds with boiling water. Add 2 oz. Old Mr. Boston Dry Gin. *Stir and decorate with slice of lemon. Grate nutmeg on top.*

Glögg
Pour following into kettle:
2 ⅘ Qts. Wine (Port, Sherry, Claret, Burgundy or Madeira)
Insert cheesecloth bag containing:
    2 oz. Dried Orange Peel
    2 oz. Cinnamon Sticks
    20 Cardamon Seeds
    25 Cloves
and boil slowly for 15 minutes, stirring occasionally. Add 1 lb. each blanched almonds and seedless raisins and continue to boil for additional 15 minutes. Remove kettle from stove and place wire grill containing 1 lb. lump sugar over opening. Pour ⅕ qt. of Old Mr. Boston Five Star Brandy over sugar making sure to saturate all of it. Then light sugar with match and let it flame. After sugar has melted replace kettle cover to extinguish flame. Stir again and remove spice bag. Serve hot in punch cups with a few almonds and raisins.

Golden Slipper Cocktail
¾ oz. Yellow Chartreuse
2 oz. Old Mr. Boston Apricot Flavored Brandy
Stir well with cracked ice and strain into 4 oz. cocktail glass. Float yolk of egg on top.

Golf Cocktail
1½ oz. Old Mr. Boston Dry Gin
¾ oz. Dry Vermouth
2 Dashes Bitters
Stir well with cracked ice and strain into 3 oz. cocktail glass.

G

Grand Royal Fizz

Juice ¼ Orange
Juice ½ Lemon
1 Teaspoon Powdered Sugar
2 oz. Old Mr. Boston Dry Gin
½ Teaspoon Maraschino
2 Teaspoons Sweet Cream
Shake well with cracked ice and strain into 8 oz. highball glass. Fill with carbonated water and stir.

Grapefruit Cocktail

1 oz. Grapefruit Juice
1 oz. Old Mr. Boston Dry Gin
1 Teaspoon Maraschino
Shake well with cracked ice and strain into 3 oz. cocktail glass. Serve with a cherry.

Grasshopper Cocktail

¾ oz. Old Mr. Boston Creme de Menthe (green)
¾ oz. Old Mr. Boston Creme de Cacao (white)
¾ oz. Light Sweet Cream
Shake well with cracked ice and strain into 3 oz. cocktail glass.

Green Dragon Cocktail

Juice of ¼ Lemon
½ oz. Old Mr. Boston Kummel
½ oz. Old Mr. Boston Creme de Menthe (Green)
1½ oz. Old Mr. Boston Dry Gin
4 Dashes Orange Bitters
Shake well with cracked ice and strain into 4 oz. cocktail glass.

Green Fizz

1 Teaspoon Powdered Sugar
White 1 Egg
Juice ½ Lemon
2 oz. Old Mr. Boston Dry Gin
1 Teaspoon Old Mr. Boston Creme de Menthe (Green)
Shake well with cracked ice and strain into 8 oz. highball glass. Fill with carbonated water and stir.

Green Swizzle

Make same as Gin Swizzle *(see page 43), and add 1 tablespoon Old Mr. Boston Green Creme de Menthe. If desired, rum, brandy or whiskey may be substituted for the gin.*

Grenadine Rickey

1 Cube of Ice
Juice ½ Lime
1½ oz. Grenadine
Fill 8 oz. highball glass with carbonated water and stir. Leave lime in glass.

Gypsy Cocktail

1¼ oz. Sweet Vermouth
1¼ oz. Old Mr. Boston Dry Gin
Stir well with cracked ice and strain into 3 oz. cocktail glass. Serve with a cherry.

Harlem Cocktail
¾ oz. Pineapple Juice
1½ oz. Old Mr. Boston Dry Gin
½ Teaspoon Maraschino
2 Cubes of Pineapple
Shake well with cracked ice and strain into 3 oz. cocktail glass.

Harry Lauder Cocktail
1¼ oz. Old Mr. Boston Scotch Whisky
1¼ oz. Sweet Vermouth
½ Teaspoon Simple Syrup
Stir well with cracked ice and strain into 3 oz. cocktail glass.

Harvard Cocktail
1½ oz. Old Mr. Boston Five Star Brandy
¾ oz. Sweet Vermouth
1 Dash Bitters
1 Teaspoon Grenadine
2 Teaspoons Lemon Juice
Shake well with cracked ice and strain into 3 oz. cocktail glass.

Harvard Cooler
Into 12 oz. Tom Collins glass put:
½ Teaspoon Powdered Sugar
2 oz. Carbonated Water
Stir. Then fill glass with cracked ice and add:
2 oz. Apple Brandy
Fill with carbonated water or ginger ale and stir again. Insert spiral of orange or lemon peel (or both) and dangle end over rim of glass.

Hasty Cocktail
¾ oz. Dry Vermouth
1½ oz. Old Mr. Boston Dry Gin
¼ Teaspoon Absinthe Substitute
1 Teaspoon Grenadine
Stir well with cracked ice and strain into 3 oz. cocktail glass.

Havana Cocktail
1¼ oz. Pineapple Juice
½ Teaspoon Lemon Juice
¾ oz. Old Mr. Boston Imported Rum
Shake well with cracked ice and strain into 3 oz. cocktail glass.

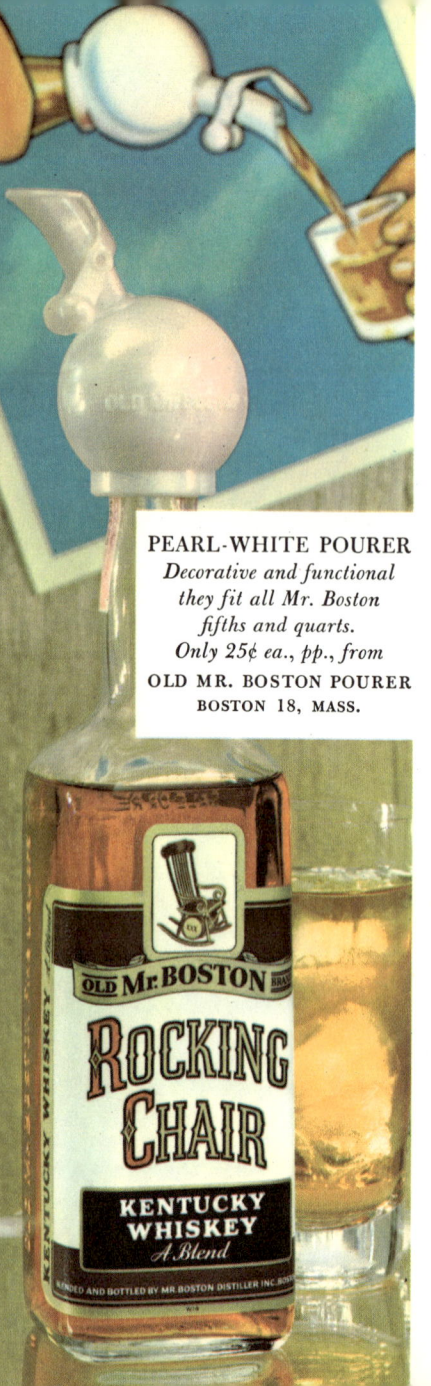

PEARL-WHITE POURER
Decorative and functional they fit all Mr. Boston fifths and quarts. Only 25¢ ea., pp., from
OLD MR. BOSTON POURER
BOSTON 18, MASS.

Hawaiian Cocktail
2 oz. Old Mr. Boston Dry Gin
½ oz. Pineapple Juice
½ oz. Curacao
Shake well with cracked ice and strain into 4 oz. cocktail glass.

Headless Horseman
Into 12 oz. Tom Collins glass, put:
2 oz. Old Mr. Boston Vodka
3 Dashes Bitters
Add several cubes of ice, fill with dry ginger ale and stir. Decorate with slice of orange.

Highballs
See Index on page 144 for complete list of HIGHBALL *recipes.*

Highland Cooler
Into 12 oz. Tom Collins glass, put:
½ Teaspoon Powdered Sugar
2 oz. Carbonated Water, and stir.
Fill glass with cracked ice and add:
2 oz. Old Mr. Boston Scotch Whisky
Fill with carbonated water or ginger ale and stir again. Insert spiral of orange or lemon peel (or both) and dangle end over rim of glass.

Highland Fling Cocktail
¾ oz. Sweet Vermouth
1½ oz. Old Mr. Boston Scotch Whisky
2 Dashes Orange Bitters
Stir well with cracked ice and strain into 3 oz. cocktail glass. Serve with an olive.

◀ Rocking Chair Kentucky Whiskey—A Blend
80 Proof 72½% Grain Neutral Spirits

H

Hill Billy Highball
1 Cube of Ice
2 ozs. Georgia Moon Corn Whiskey
Fill 8 oz. highball glass with Mountain Dew.
Then add twist of lemon peel if desired and stir.

Hoffman House Cocktail
¾ oz. Dry Vermouth
1½ oz. Old Mr. Boston Dry Gin
2 Dashes Orange Bitters
Stir well with cracked ice and strain into 3 oz. cocktail glass. Serve with an olive.

Hole-in-One Cocktail
1½ oz. Old Mr. Boston Scotch Whisky
¾ oz. Dry Vermouth
¼ Teaspoon Lemon Juice
1 Dash Orange Bitters
Shake well with cracked ice and strain into 3 oz. cocktail glass.

Homestead Cocktail
1½ oz. Old Mr. Boston Dry Gin
¾ oz. Sweet Vermouth
Stir well with cracked ice and strain into 3 oz. cocktail glass and serve with slice of orange.

Honeymoon Cocktail
¾ oz. Benedictine
¾ oz. Apple Brandy
Juice of ½ Lemon
1 Teaspoon Curacao
Shake well with cracked ice and strain into 3 oz. cocktail glass.

Honolulu Cocktail No. 1
1 Dash Bitters
¼ Teaspoon Orange Juice
¼ Teaspoon Pineapple Juice
¼ Teaspoon Lemon Juice
½ Teaspoon Powdered Sugar
1½ oz. Old Mr. Boston Dry Gin
Shake well with cracked ice and strain into 3 oz. cocktail glass.

Honolulu Cocktail No. 2
¾ oz. Old Mr. Boston Dry Gin
¾ oz. Maraschino
¾ oz. Benedictine
Stir well with cracked ice and strain into 3 oz. cocktail glass.

Hoot Mon Cocktail
¾ oz. Sweet Vermouth
1½ oz. Old Mr. Boston Scotch Whisky
1 Teaspoon Benedictine
Stir well with cracked ice and strain into 3 oz. cocktail glass. Twist of lemon peel and drop in glass.

Hop Toad Cocktail
Juice ½ Lime
¾ oz. Old Mr. Boston Apricot Flavored Brandy
¾ oz. Old Mr. Boston Imported Rum
Stir well with cracked ice and strain into 3 oz. cocktail glass.

Horses Neck (With a Kick)
Peel rind of whole lemon in spiral fashion and put in 12 oz. Tom Collins glass with one end hanging over the rim. Fill glass with ice cubes. Add 2 oz. Old Mr. Boston Whiskey.* *Then fill with ginger ale and stir well.*

---

* *Bourbon, Blended, Rye or Canadian.*

H

Hot Brandy Flip

1 Egg
1 Teaspoon Powdered Sugar
1½ oz. Old Mr. Boston Five Star Brandy
Beat egg, sugar and brandy and pour into Tom & Jerry Mug and fill with hot milk. Grate nutmeg on top.

Hot Brick Toddy

Into hot whiskey glass, put:
1 Teaspoon Butter
1 Teaspoon Powdered Sugar
3 Pinches Cinnamon
1 oz. Hot Water
Dissolve thoroughly. Then add:
1½ oz. Old Mr. Boston Whiskey*
Fill with boiling water and stir.

Hot Buttered Rum

Put lump of sugar into hot whiskey glass and fill two-thirds with boiling water. Add square of butter and 2 oz. Old Mr. Boston Imported Rum. Stir and grate nutmeg on top.

Hot Buttered Wine

For each serving—heat ½ cup Muscatel Wine. Add ¼ cup water just to simmering; do not boil. Preheat mug or cup with boiling water. Pour heated wine mixture into mug and add 1 teaspoon butter and 2 teaspoons maple syrup. Stir well and sprinkle nutmeg on top. Serve at once.

Hot Drinks

See Index on page 144 for complete list of Hot Drink Recipes.

Hot Springs Cocktail

1½ oz. Dry White Wine
½ oz. Pineapple Juice
½ Teaspoon Maraschino
1 Dash Orange Bitters
Shake well with cracked ice and strain into 3 oz. cocktail glass.

Hotel Plaza Cocktail

¾ oz. Sweet Vermouth
¾ oz. Dry Vermouth
¾ oz. Old Mr. Boston Dry Gin
Crush 1 Slice of Pineapple
Stir well with cracked ice and strain into 3 oz. cocktail glass.

H. P. W. Cocktail

¼ oz. Dry Vermouth
¼ oz. Sweet Vermouth
1½ oz. Old Mr. Boston Dry Gin
Stir well with cracked ice and strain into 3 oz. cocktail glass. Twist of orange peel and drop in glass.

Hula-Hula Cocktail

¾ oz. Orange Juice
1½ oz. Old Mr. Boston Dry Gin
¼ Teaspoon Powdered Sugar
Shake well with cracked ice and strain into 3 oz. cocktail glass.

Huntsman Cocktail

1½ oz. Old Mr. Boston Vodka
½ oz. Jamaica Rum
Juice of ½ Lime
Powdered sugar to taste
Shake well with cracked ice and strain into 3 oz. cocktail glass.

* *Bourbon, Blended, Rye or Canadian.*

I

Ice Cream Flip
1 Egg
1 oz. Maraschino
1 oz. Curacao
1 Small Scoop Vanilla Ice Cream
Shake well with cracked ice and strain into 5 oz. flip glass. Grate a little nutmeg on top.

Ideal Cocktail
1 oz. Dry Vermouth
1 oz. Old Mr. Boston Dry Gin
¼ Teaspoon Maraschino
½ Teaspoon Grapefruit or Lemon Juice
Shake well with cracked ice and strain into 3 oz. cocktail glass. Serve with a cherry.

Imperial Cocktail
1¼ oz. Dry Vermouth
1¼ oz. Old Mr. Boston Dry Gin
¼ Teaspoon Maraschino
1 Dash Bitters
Stir well with cracked ice and strain into 3 oz. cocktail glass. Serve with a cherry.

Imperial Fizz
Juice of ½ Lemon
½ oz. Old Mr. Boston Imported Rum
1½ oz. Old Mr. Boston Whiskey*
1 Teaspoon Powdered Sugar
Shake well with cracked ice and strain into 7 oz. highball glass. Fill with carbonated water and stir.

Income Tax Cocktail
¼ oz. Dry Vermouth
¼ oz. Sweet Vermouth
1 oz. Old Mr. Boston Dry Gin
1 Dash Bitters
Juice of ¼ Orange
Shake well with cracked ice and strain into 3 oz. cocktail glass.

Irish Coffee
Into a pre-warmed 8 oz. stemmed glass (or coffee cup), pour 1½ oz. Irish Whiskey. Add 1 or 2 teaspoons sugar and fill to within ½ inch of top with strong, very hot black coffee. Stir to dissolve sugar. Float to brim with chilled whipped cream. Do not stir. Drink through floating cream.

* *Bourbon, Blended, Rye or Canadian.*

J

Irish Rickey
1 Cube of Ice
Juice of ½ Lime
1½ oz. Irish Whiskey
Fill 8 oz. highball glass with carbonated water and stir. Leave lime in glass.

Irish Shillelagh
Juice ½ Lemon
1 Teaspoon Powdered Sugar
1½ oz. Irish Whiskey
½ oz. Old Mr. Boston Sloe Gin
½ oz. Old Mr. Boston Imported Rum
2 Slices of Peach
Shake well with cracked ice and strain into 5 oz. punch glass. Decorate with fresh raspberries, strawberries and a cherry.

Irish Whiskey Cocktail
½ Teaspoon Curacao
½ Teaspoon Absinthe Substitute
¼ Teaspoon Maraschino
1 Dash Bitters
2 oz. Irish Whiskey
Stir well with cracked ice and strain into 3 oz. cocktail glass. Serve with an olive.

Irish Whiskey Highball
1 Cube of Ice
2 oz. Irish Whiskey
Fill 8 oz. highball glass with ginger ale or carbonated water. Add twist of lemon peel, if desired, and stir.

Jack-in-the-Box Cocktail
1 oz. Apple Brandy
1 oz. Pineapple Juice
Dash of Bitters
Shake well with cracked ice and strain into 3 oz. cocktail glass.

Jack Rose Cocktail
1½ oz. Apple Brandy
Juice ½ Lime
1 Teaspoon Grenadine
Shake well with cracked ice and strain into 3 oz. cocktail glass.

Jamaica Glow Cocktail
1 oz. Old Mr. Boston Dry Gin
½ oz. Claret
½ oz. Orange Juice
1 Teaspoon Jamaica Rum
Shake well with cracked ice and strain into 3 oz. cocktail glass.

Jamaica Granito
Small scoop of either Lemon or Orange Sherbet
1½ oz. Old Mr. Boston Five Star Brandy
1 oz. Curacao
Use 12 oz. Tom Collins glass and fill balance with carbonated water and stir. Grate nutmeg on top.

Japanese Fizz
Juice ½ Lemon
1 Teaspoon Powdered Sugar
1½ oz. Old Mr. Boston Whiskey*
½ oz. Port Wine
White 1 Egg
Shake well with cracked ice and strain into 8 oz. highball glass. Fill with carbonated water and stir. Serve with slice of pineapple.

Jersey Lightning Cocktail
1½ oz. Apple Brandy
½ oz. Sweet Vermouth
Juice 1 Lime
Shake well with cracked ice and strain into 3½ oz. cocktail glass.

* *Bourbon, Blended, Rye or Canadian.*

ottled-in-Bond Bourbon and Rye 100 Proof 4 Years Old
▶

J

Jewel Cocktail

¾ oz. Green Chartreuse
¾ oz. Sweet Vermouth
¾ oz. Old Mr. Boston Dry Gin
1 Dash Orange Bitters
Stir well with cracked ice and strain into 3 oz. cocktail glass. Serve with a cherry.

Jeyplak Cocktail

1½ oz. Old Mr. Boston Dry Gin
¾ oz. Sweet Vermouth
¼ Teaspoon Absinthe Substitute
Stir well with cracked ice and strain into 3 oz. cocktail glass. Serve with a cherry.

Jockey Club Cocktail

1 Dash Bitters
¼ Teaspoon Old Mr. Boston Creme de Cacao
Juice of ¼ Lemon
1½ oz. Old Mr. Boston Dry Gin
Shake well with cracked ice and strain into 3 oz. cocktail glass.

John Collins

Juice ½ Lemon
1 Teaspoon Powdered Sugar
2 oz. Holland Gin
Shake well with cracked ice and strain into 12 oz. Tom Collins glass. Add several cubes of ice, fill with carbonated water and stir. Decorate with slice of orange, lemon and a cherry. Serve with straws.

Johnnie Cocktail

¾ oz. Curacao
1½ oz. Old Mr. Boston Sloe Gin
1 Teaspoon Old Mr. Boston Anisette
Stir well with cracked ice and strain into 3 oz. cocktail glass.

Journalist Cocktail

¼ oz. Dry Vermouth
¼ oz. Sweet Vermouth
1½ oz. Old Mr. Boston Dry Gin
½ Teaspoon Lemon Juice
½ Teaspoon Curacao
1 Dash Bitters
Shake well with cracked ice and strain into 3 oz. cocktail glass.

Judge Jr. Cocktail

¾ oz. Old Mr. Boston Dry Gin
¾ oz. Old Mr. Boston Imported Rum
Juice of ¼ Lemon
½ Teaspoon Powdered Sugar
¼ Teaspoon Grenadine
Shake well with cracked ice and strain into 3 oz. cocktail glass.

Judgette Cocktail

¾ oz. Old Mr. Boston Peach Flavored Brandy
¾ oz. Old Mr. Boston Dry Gin
¾ oz. Dry Vermouth
Juice of ¼ Lime
Shake well with cracked ice and strain into 3 oz. cocktail glass. Serve with a cherry.

Juleps

See Index on page 144 for complete list of Julep *recipes.*

Kangaroo Cocktail

1½ oz. Old Mr. Boston Vodka
¾ oz. Dry Vermouth
Stir well with cracked ice and strain into 3 oz. cocktail glass. Serve with twist of lemon peel.

K. C. B. Cocktail

½ oz. Old Mr. Boston Kummel
1½ oz. Old Mr. Boston Dry Gin
¼ Teaspoon Old Mr. Boston Apricot Flavored Brandy
¼ Teaspoon Lemon Juice
Shake well with cracked ice and strain into 3 oz. cocktail glass. Add twist of lemon peel and drop in glass.

Kentucky Cocktail

1½ oz. Pineapple Juice
¾ oz. Old Mr. Boston Kentucky Bourbon Whiskey
Shake well with cracked ice and strain into 3 oz. cocktail glass.

Kentucky Colonel Cocktail

½ oz. Benedictine
1½ oz. Old Mr. Boston Kentucky Bourbon Whiskey
Twist of Lemon Peel
Stir well with cracked ice and strain into a 3 oz. cocktail glass.

King Cole Cocktail

1 Slice of Orange
1 Slice of Pineapple
½ Teaspoon Powdered Sugar
Muddle well in Old Fashioned cocktail glass and add:
2 oz. Old Mr. Boston Whiskey*
1 Cube of Ice
Stir well.

* *Bourbon, Blended, Rye or Canadian.*

OLD
Mr. BOSTON
Distilled
DRY
GIN
OLD Mr. BOSTON
DELUXE
DRY
GIN
DISTILLED
Eighty Proof -
just like in England
DISTILLED FROM 100% GRAIN NEUTRAL SPIRITS

K

Kiss-in-the-Dark Cocktail
¾ oz. Old Mr. Boston Dry Gin
¾ oz. Old Mr. Boston Wild Cherry Flavored Brandy
¾ oz. Dry Vermouth
Stir well with cracked ice and strain into 3 oz. cocktail glass.

Klondike Cooler
Into 12 oz. Tom Collins glass, put:
½ Teaspoon Powdered Sugar
2 oz. Carbonated Water
Stir and fill glass with cracked ice and add:
2 oz. Old Mr. Boston Whiskey*
Fill with carbonated water or ginger ale and stir again. Insert spiral of orange or lemon peel (or both) and dangle end over rim of glass.

Knickerbocker Cocktail
¼ Teaspoon Sweet Vermouth
¾ oz. Dry Vermouth
1½ oz. Old Mr. Boston Dry Gin
Stir well with cracked ice, strain into 3 oz. glass. Add twist of lemon peel and drop in glass.

Knickerbocker Special Cocktail
1 Teaspoon Raspberry Syrup
1 Teaspoon Lemon Juice
1 Teaspoon Orange Juice
2 oz. Old Mr. Boston Imported Rum
½ Teaspoon Curacao
Shake well with cracked ice and strain into 4 oz. cocktail glass. Decorate with small slice of pineapple.

Knock-out Cocktail
½ oz. Absinthe Substitute
¾ oz. Old Mr. Boston Dry Gin
¾ oz. Dry Vermouth
1 Teaspoon Old Mr. Boston Creme de Menthe (white)
Stir well with cracked ice and strain into 3 oz. cocktail glass. Serve with a cherry.

Kretchma Cocktail
1 oz. Old Mr. Boston Vodka
1 oz. Old Mr. Boston Creme de Cacao
½ oz. Lemon Juice
1 Dash Grenadine
Shake well with cracked ice and strain into 3 oz. cocktail glass.

Kup's Indispensable Cocktail
½ oz. Sweet Vermouth
½ oz. Dry Vermouth
1¼ oz. Old Mr. Boston Dry Gin
1 Dash Bitters
Stir well with cracked ice and strain into 3 oz. cocktail glass.

---

* Bourbon, Blended, Rye or Canadian.

80 Proof 100% Grain Neutral Spirits

L

LADIES' COCKTAIL

1¾ oz. Old Mr. Boston Whiskey*
½ Teaspoon Absinthe Substitute
½ Teaspoon Old Mr. Boston Anisette
2 Dashes Bitters
Stir well with cracked ice and strain into 3 oz. cocktail glass. Serve with a piece of pineapple on top.

LADY LOVE FIZZ

1 Teaspoon Powdered Sugar
Juice of ½ Lemon
White of 1 Egg
2 oz. Old Mr. Boston Dry Gin
2 Teaspoons Sweet Cream
Shake well with cracked ice and strain into 8 oz. highball glass. Fill with carbonated water and stir.

LASKY COCKTAIL

¾ oz. Grape Juice
¾ oz. Swedish Punch
¾ oz. Old Mr. Boston Dry Gin
Shake well with cracked ice and strain into 3 oz. cocktail glass.

LAWHILL COCKTAIL

¾ oz. Dry Vermouth
1½ oz. Old Mr. Boston Whiskey*
¼ Teaspoon Absinthe Substitute
¼ Teaspoon Maraschino
1 Dash Bitters
Stir well with cracked ice and strain into 3 oz. cocktail glass.

LEAP FROG HIGHBALL

Juice ½ Lemon
2 oz. Old Mr. Boston Dry Gin
1 Cube of Ice
Fill 8 oz. highball glass with ginger ale and stir gently.

LEAP YEAR COCKTAIL

1¼ oz. Old Mr. Boston Dry Gin
½ oz. Old Mr. Boston Orange Flavored Gin
½ oz. Sweet Vermouth
¼ Teaspoon Lemon Juice
Shake well with cracked ice and strain into 3 oz. cocktail glass.

* Bourbon, Blended, Rye or Canadian

L

Leave It to Me Cocktail No. 1

½ oz. Old Mr. Boston Apricot Flavored Brandy
½ oz. Dry Vermouth
1 oz. Old Mr. Boston Dry Gin
¼ Teaspoon Lemon Juice
¼ Teaspoon Grenadine
Shake well with cracked ice and strain into 3 oz. cocktail glass.

Leave It to Me Cocktail No. 2

1 Teaspoon Raspberry Syrup
1 Teaspoon Lemon Juice
¼ Teaspoon Maraschino
1½ oz. Old Mr. Boston Dry Gin
Stir well with cracked ice and strain into 3 oz. cocktail glass.

Lemon Squash

1 Lemon, peeled and quartered
2 Teaspoons Powdered Sugar
Muddle well in 12 oz. Tom Collins glass until juice is well extracted. Then fill glass with cracked ice. Add carbonated water and stir. Decorate with fruits.

Lemonade (Carbonated)

2 Teaspoons Powdered Sugar
Juice 1 Lemon
Stir. Then fill 12 oz. Tom Collins glass with shaved ice. Add enough carbonated water to fill glass and stir. Decorate with slice of orange, lemon and a cherry. Serve with straws.

Lemonade (Claret)

2 Teaspoons Powdered Sugar
Juice 1 Lemon
Stir. Then fill 12 oz. Tom Collins glass with shaved ice. Add enough water to fill glass, leaving room to float 2 oz. Claret. Decorate with slice of orange, lemon and a cherry. Serve with straws.

Lemonade (Egg)

Juice 1 Lemon
2 Teaspoons Powdered Sugar
1 Whole Egg
Shake well and strain into 12 oz. Tom Collins glass filled with shaved ice. Add enough water to fill glass. Serve with straws.

Lemonade (Fruit)

Juice 1 Lemon
2 Teaspoons Powdered Sugar
1 oz. Raspberry Syrup
Stir. Then fill 12 oz. Tom Collins glass with shaved ice. Add enough water to fill glass and stir. Decorate with a slice of orange, lemon and a cherry. Serve with straws.

Lemonade (Golden)

Juice 1 Lemon
2 Teaspoons Powdered Sugar
Yolk of 1 Egg
6 oz. Water
Shake well with cracked ice and strain into 12 oz. Tom Collins glass. Decorate with a slice of orange, lemon and a cherry.

OLD Mr. BOSTON
CREAMY TOP
OLD Mr. BOSTON
Sloe Gin
FOR THE PERFECT "FIZZ"
OLD Mr. BOSTON Fine Liquors
Old Mr. BOSTON
ORANGE FLAVORED GIN
OLD Mr. BOSTON Fine Liquors
Old Mr. BOSTON
MINT FLAVORED GIN
"Try a Mint Tom Collins"

L

Lemonade (Modern)
2 Teaspoons Powdered Sugar
1½ oz. Sherry Wine
1 oz. Old Mr. Boston Sloe Gin
Cut lemon in quarters and muddle well with sugar. Add sherry and sloe gin. Shake well with cracked ice and strain into 12 oz. Tom Collins glass. Fill glass with carbonated water.

Lemonade (Plain)
2 Teaspoons Powdered Sugar
Juice 1 Lemon
Stir. Then fill 12 oz. Tom Collins glass with shaved ice. Add enough water to fill glass and stir well. Decorate with slice of orange, lemon and a cherry.

Liberty Cocktail
¾ oz. Old Mr. Boston Imported Rum
1½ oz. Apple Brandy
¼ Teaspoon Simple Syrup
Stir well with cracked ice and strain into 3 oz. cocktail glass.

Limeade
Juice 3 Limes
3 Teaspoons Powdered Sugar
Fill 12 oz. Tom Collins glass with shaved ice. Add enough water to fill glass. Stir well and drop lime in glass. Add a cherry. Serve with straws.

Linstead Cocktail
1 oz. Old Mr. Boston Whiskey*
1 oz. Pineapple Juice
½ Teaspoon Powdered Sugar
¼ Teaspoon Absinthe Substitute
¼ Teaspoon Lemon Juice
Shake well with cracked ice and strain into 3 oz. cocktail glass.

* *Bourbon, Blended, Rye or Canadian.*

Little Devil Cocktail
Juice of ¼ Lemon
¼ oz. Triple Sec
¾ oz. Old Mr. Boston Imported Rum
¾ oz. Old Mr. Boston Dry Gin
Shake well with cracked ice and strain into 3 oz. cocktail glass.

Little Princess Cocktail
1¼ oz. Sweet Vermouth
1¼ oz. Old Mr. Boston Imported Rum
Stir well with cracked ice and strain into 3 oz. cocktail glass.

London Buck
1 Cube of Ice
2 oz. Old Mr. Boston Dry Gin
Juice of ½ Lemon
Fill 8 oz. highball glass with ginger ale and stir gently.

London Cocktail
2 oz. Old Mr. Boston Dry Gin
2 Dashes Orange Bitters
½ Teaspoon Simple Syrup
½ Teaspoon Maraschino
Stir well with cracked ice and strain into 3 oz. cocktail glass. Add twist of lemon peel to glass.

London Special Cocktail
Put rind of ½ orange into 6 oz. Champagne glass. Add:
1 Lump Sugar
2 Dashes Bitters
Fill with Champagne, well chilled, and stir gently.

Sloe Gin, Mint and Orange Flavored Gins 70 Proof

L

Lone Tree Cocktail

¾ oz. Sweet Vermouth
1½ oz. Old Mr. Boston Dry Gin
Stir well with cracked ice and strain into 3 oz. cocktail glass.

Lone Tree Cooler

Into 12 oz. Tom Collins glass, put:
½ Teaspoon Powdered Sugar
2 oz. Carbonated Water
Stir and fill glass with cracked ice and add:
2 oz. Old Mr. Boston Dry Gin
½ oz. Dry Vermouth
Fill with carbonated water or ginger ale and stir again. Insert spiral of orange or lemon peel (or both) and dangle end over rim of glass.

Los Angeles Cocktail

Juice of ½ Lemon
1 Teaspoon Powdered Sugar
1 Egg
¼ Teaspoon Sweet Vermouth
1½ oz. Old Mr. Boston Whiskey*
Shake well with cracked ice and strain into 4 oz. cocktail glass.

Love Cocktail

2 oz. Old Mr. Boston Sloe Gin
White of 1 Egg
½ Teaspoon Lemon Juice
½ Teaspoon Raspberry Juice
Shake well with cracked ice and strain into 4 oz. cocktail glass.

Loving Cup

Use large Glass Pitcher.
4 Teaspoons Powdered Sugar
6 oz. Carbonated Water
1 oz. Triple Sec
2 oz. Old Mr. Boston Five Star Brandy
Fill pitcher with cubes of ice. Add 1 pint Claret. Stir well and decorate with as many fruits as available and also rind of cucumber inserted on each side of pitcher. Top with small bunch of mint sprigs.

Luxury Cocktail

3 oz. Old Mr. Boston Five Star Brandy
2 Dashes Orange Bitters
3 oz. well chilled Champagne
Stir very gently. Use 6 oz. Saucer Champagne glass.

* *Bourbon, Blended, Rye or Canadian*

Maiden's Blush Cocktail

¼ Teaspoon Lemon Juice
1 Teaspoon Curacao
1 Teaspoon Grenadine
1½ oz. Old Mr. Boston Dry Gin
Shake well with cracked ice and strain into 3 oz. cocktail glass.

Mai-Tai

½ Teaspoon Powdered Sugar
2 oz. Old Mr. Boston Imported Rum
1 oz. Curacao
½ oz. Orgeat or any almond flavored syrup
½ oz. Grenadine
½ oz. Fresh Lime Juice
Shake well with cracked ice and strain into large Old Fashioned cocktail glass about ⅓ full with crushed ice. Decorate with Maraschino cherry speared to wedge of preferably fresh pineapple. For a hair raiser top with a dash of 151 proof rum and for a real Hawaiian effect float an orchid on each drink. Serve with straws.

Major Bailey

¼ oz. Lime Juice
¼ oz. Lemon Juice
½ Teaspoon Powdered Sugar
12 Mint Leaves
Muddle well and pour into 12 oz. Tom Collins glass filled with shaved ice, and add: 2 oz. Old Mr. Boston Dry Gin. Stir gently, until glass is frosted. Decorate with spring of mint and serve with straws.

Mamie Gilroy

Juice ½ Lime
2 Cubes of Ice
2 oz. Old Mr. Boston Scotch Whisky
1 Dash Bitters
Fill 12 oz. Tom Collins glass with carbonated water and stir gently.

Mamie Taylor

Juice ½ Lime
2 Cubes of Ice
2 oz. Old Mr. Boston Scotch Whisky
Fill 12 oz. Tom Collins glass with ginger ale and stir gently.

M

Mamie's Sister
Juice 1 Lime
Drop rind in glass.
2 Cubes of Ice
2 oz. Old Mr. Boston Dry Gin
Fill 12 oz. Tom Collins glass with ginger ale and stir gently.

Manhattan Cocktail
1 Dash Bitters
¾ oz. Sweet Vermouth
1½ oz. Old Mr. Boston Whiskey*
Stir well with cracked ice and strain into 3 oz. cocktail glass. Serve with a cherry.

Manhattan Cocktail (Dry)
1 Dash Bitters
¾ oz. Dry Vermouth
1½ oz. Old Mr. Boston Whiskey*
Stir well with cracked ice and strain into 3 oz. cocktail glass. Serve with an olive.

Manhattan Cocktail (Sweet)
1 Dash Bitters
¾ oz. Sweet Vermouth
1½ oz. Old Mr. Boston Whiskey*
Stir well with cracked ice and strain into 3 oz. cocktail glass. Serve with a cherry.

Manila Fizz
2 oz. Old Mr. Boston Dry Gin
1 Egg
1 Teaspoon Powdered Sugar
2 oz. Sarsaparilla
Juice of 1 Lime or ½ Lemon
Shake well with cracked ice and strain into 10 oz. Pilsner glass.

Margarita Cocktail
1½ oz. Tequila
½ oz. Triple Sec
Juice of ½ Lemon or Lime
Stir with crushed ice. Rub rim of 3 oz. cocktail glass with rind of lemon or lime, dip rim in salt, pour and serve.

Martinez Cocktail
1 Dash Orange Bitters
1 oz. Dry Vermouth
¼ Teaspoon Curacao
1 oz. Old Mr. Boston Dry Gin
Stir well with cracked ice and strain into 3 oz. cocktail glass. Serve with a cherry.

Martini Cocktail
See *Special Martini Section* on pages 116 and 117.

Mary Garden Cocktail
1½ oz. Dubonnet
¾ oz. Dry Vermouth
Stir well with cracked ice and strain into 3 oz. cocktail glass.

Mary Pickford Cocktail
1 oz. Old Mr. Boston Imported Rum
1 oz. Pineapple Juice
¼ Teaspoon Grenadine
¼ Teaspoon Maraschino
Shake well with cracked ice and strain into 3 oz. cocktail glass.

*Bourbon, Blended, Rye or Canadian.

M

MAURICE COCKTAIL
Juice of ¼ Orange
½ oz. Sweet Vermouth
½ oz. Dry Vermouth
1 oz. Old Mr. Boston Dry Gin
1 Dash Bitters
Shake well with cracked ice and strain into 4 oz. cocktail glass.

MAY BLOSSOM FIZZ
1 Teaspoon Grenadine
Juice ½ Lemon
2 oz. Swedish Punch
Shake well with cracked ice and strain into 7 oz. highball glass. Fill with carbonated water and stir.

McCLELLAND COCKTAIL
¾ oz. Curacao
1½ oz. Old Mr. Boston Sloe Gin
1 Dash Orange Bitters
Shake well with cracked ice and strain into 3 oz. cocktail glass.

MELON COCKTAIL
2 oz. Old Mr. Boston Dry Gin
¼ Teaspoon Lemon Juice
¼ Teaspoon Maraschino
Shake well with cracked ice and strain into 3 oz. cocktail glass. Serve with a cherry.

MERRY WIDOW COCKTAIL No. 1
1¼ oz. Old Mr. Boston Dry Gin
1¼ oz. Dry Vermouth
½ Teaspoon Benedictine
½ Teaspoon Absinthe Substitute
1 Dash Orange Bitters
Stir well with cracked ice and strain into 3 oz. cocktail glass. Add twist of lemon peel and drop in glass.

MERRY WIDOW COCKTAIL No. 2
1¼ oz. Maraschino
1¼ oz. Old Mr. Boston Wild Cherry Flavored Brandy
Stir well with cracked ice and strain into 3 oz. cocktail glass. Serve with a cherry.

MERRY WIDOW FIZZ
Juice ½ Orange
Juice ½ Lemon
White of 1 Egg
1 Teaspoon Powdered Sugar
1½ oz. Old Mr. Boston Sloe Gin
Shake well with cracked ice and strain into 8 oz. highball glass. Fill with carbonated water and stir.

METROPOLITAN COCKTAIL
1¼ oz. Old Mr. Boston Five Star Brandy
1¼ oz. Sweet Vermouth
½ Teaspoon Simple Syrup
1 Dash Bitters
Stir well with cracked ice and strain into 3 oz. cocktail glass.

MEXICOLA
2 oz. Tequila
Juice ½ Lime
Use 12 oz. Tom Collins glass with cubes of ice. Fill balance with cola and stir gently.

M

Miami Beach Cocktail

¾ oz. Old Mr. Boston Scotch Whisky
¾ oz. Dry Vermouth
¾ oz. Grapefruit Juice
Stir well with cracked ice and strain into 3 oz. cocktail glass.

Midnight Cocktail

1 oz. Old Mr. Boston Apricot Flavored Brandy
½ oz. Curacao
½ oz. Lemon Juice
Shake well with cracked ice and strain into 3 oz. cocktail glass.

Mikado Cocktail

2 oz. Old Mr. Boston Five Star Brandy
2 Dashes Bitters
½ Teaspoon Old Mr. Boston Creme de Cacao
½ Teaspoon Curacao
Shake well with cracked ice and strain into 3 oz. cocktail glass.

Milk Punch

1 Teaspoon Powdered Sugar
2 oz. Old Mr. Boston Whiskey*
½ pt. Milk
Shake well with cracked ice and strain into 12 oz. Tom Collins glass. Grate nutmeg on top.

Million Dollar Cocktail

2 Teaspoons Pineapple Juice
1 Teaspoon Grenadine
White of 1 Egg
¾ oz. Sweet Vermouth
1½ oz. Old Mr. Boston Dry Gin
Shake well with cracked ice and strain into 4 oz. cocktail glass.

Millionaire Cocktail

White of 1 Egg
¼ Teaspoon Grenadine
½ oz. Curacao
1½ oz. Old Mr. Boston Whiskey*
Shake well with cracked ice and strain into 4 oz. cocktail glass.

Mint Collins

Juice ½ Lemon
2 oz. Old Mr. Boston Mint Flavored Gin
Shake well with cracked ice and strain into 12 oz. Tom Collins glass. Add several cubes of ice, fill with carbonated water and stir. Decorate with slice of lemon, orange and a cherry. Serve with straws.

Mint Gin Cocktail

1 oz. Old Mr. Boston Mint Flavored Gin
1 oz. White Port Wine
¼ oz. Dry Vermouth
Stir well with cracked ice and strain into 3 oz. cocktail glass.

Mint Highball

1 Cube of Ice
2 oz. Old Mr. Boston Creme de Menthe (green)
Fill 8 oz. highball glass with ginger ale or carbonated water. Add twist of lemon peel, if desired, and stir.

* *Bourbon, Blended, Rye or Canadian.*

M

Mint Julep

Into Silver Mug or 12 oz. Tom Collins glass put:
4 Sprigs of Mint
1 Teaspoon Powdered Sugar
2 Teaspoons of Water, and muddle
Fill glass or mug with shaved ice, add 2½ oz. Old Mr. Boston Kentucky Straight Bourbon Whiskey, and stir gently until glass is frosted. Decorate with slice of orange, lemon, pineapple and a cherry Insert 5 or 6 sprigs of mint on top. Serve with straws.

Mint Julep (Southern Style)

Into a silver mug or 12 ounce Tom Collins glass, dissolve 1 teaspoon powdered sugar with 2 teaspoons of water. Then fill with finely shaved ice and add 2½ ozs. Old Mr. Boston Kentucky Straight Bourbon Whiskey. Stir until glass is heavily frosted adding more ice if necessary. (Do not hold glass with hand while stirring.) Decorate with 5 or 6 sprigs of fresh mint so that the tops are about 2 inches above rim of mug or glass. Use short straws so that it will be necessary to bury nose in mint. The mint is intended for odor rather than taste.

Mint on Rocks

Pour 2 oz. Old Mr. Boston Creme de Menthe (green) *on ice cubes in Old Fashioned cocktail glass.*

Mr. Manhattan Cocktail

Muddle lump of sugar and
4 Sprigs of Mint
¼ Teaspoon Lemon Juice
1 Teaspoon Orange Juice
1½ oz. Old Mr. Boston Dry Gin
Shake well with cracked ice and strain into 3 oz. cocktail glass.

Modern Cocktail

1½ oz. Old Mr. Boston Scotch Whisky
½ Teaspoon Lemon Juice
¼ Teaspoon Absinthe Substitute
½ Teaspoon Jamaica Rum
1 Dash Orange Bitters
Shake well with cracked ice and strain into 3 oz. cocktail glass. Serve with a cherry.

Monte Carlo Imperial Highball

2 oz. Old Mr. Boston Dry Gin
½ oz. Old Mr. Boston Creme de Menthe (white)
Juice ¼ Lemon
Shake well with cracked ice and strain into 8 oz. highball glass. Fill glass with Champagne and stir.

Montmartre Cocktail

1¼ oz. Old Mr. Boston Dry Gin
½ oz. Sweet Vermouth
½ oz. Triple Sec
Stir well with cracked ice and strain into 3 oz. cocktail glass. Serve with a cherry.

M

Morning Cocktail
1 oz. Old Mr. Boston Five Star Brandy
1 oz. Dry Vermouth
¼ Teaspoon Curacao
¼ Teaspoon Maraschino
¼ Teaspoon Absinthe Substitute
2 Dashes Orange Bitters
Stir well with cracked ice and strain into 3 oz. cocktail glass. Serve with a cherry.

Morning Glory Fizz
Juice ½ Lemon or 1 Lime
1 Teaspoon Powdered Sugar
White of 1 Egg
½ Teaspoon Absinthe Substitute
2 oz. Old Mr. Boston Scotch Whisky
Shake well with cracked ice and strain into 8 oz. highball glass. Fill with carbonated water and stir.

Moscow Mule
Into a Copper Mug, put:
1½ oz. Old Mr. Boston Vodka
Juice of ½ Lime
Add ice cubes and fill with ginger beer. Drop lime in mug to decorate.

Moulin Rouge Cocktail
1½ oz. Old Mr. Boston Sloe Gin
¾ oz. Sweet Vermouth
1 Dash Bitters
Stir well with cracked ice and strain into 3 oz. cocktail glass.

Mountain Cocktail
White of 1 Egg
¼ Teaspoon Lemon Juice
¼ Teaspoon Dry Vermouth
¼ Teaspoon Sweet Vermouth
1½ oz. Old Mr. Boston Whiskey*
Shake well with cracked ice and strain into 4 oz. cocktail glass.

Mulled Claret
Into a metal mug put:
1 Lump Sugar
Juice ½ Lemon
1 Dash Bitters
1 Teaspoon Mixed Cinnamon and Nutmeg
5 oz. Claret
Heat poker red hot and hold in liquid until boiling and serve.

* *Bourbon, Blended, Rye or Canadian.*

Napoleon Cocktail
2 oz. Old Mr. Boston Dry Gin
½ Teaspoon Curacao
½ Teaspoon Dubonnet
Stir well with cracked ice and strain into 3 oz. cocktail glass.

Negronis
¾ oz. Old Mr. Boston Dry Gin
¾ oz. Campari Bitters
¾ oz. Sweet or Dry Vermouth
¾ oz. Soda Water
Pour over ice cubes in Old Fashioned cocktail glass and stir lightly.

Nevada Cocktail
1½ oz. Old Mr. Boston Imported Rum
1 oz. Grapefruit Juice
Juice of 1 Lime
1 Dash Bitters
3 Teaspoons Powdered Sugar
Shake well with cracked ice and strain into 4 oz. cocktail glass.

New Orleans Gin Fizz
Juice ½ Lemon
Juice ½ Lime (optional)
1 Teaspoon Powdered Sugar
White of 1 Egg
2 oz. Old Mr. Boston Dry Gin
1 Tablespoon Sweet Cream
½ Teaspoon Orange Flower Water
Shake well with cracked ice and strain into 12 oz. Tom Collins glass. Fill with carbonated water and stir.

New York Cocktail
Juice 1 Lime or ½ Lemon
1 Teaspoon Powdered Sugar
1½ oz. Old Mr. Boston Whiskey*
½ Teaspoon Grenadine
Twist of Orange Peel
Shake well with cracked ice and strain into 3 oz. cocktail glass. Add twist of lemon peel and drop in glass.

New York Sour
Juice ½ Lemon
1 Teaspoon Powdered Sugar
2 oz. Old Mr. Boston Whiskey*
Shake well with cracked ice and strain into 6 oz. sour glass, leaving about ½ inch on which to float claret. Decorate with a half-slice of lemon and a cherry.

---

* *Bourbon, Blended, Rye or Canadian.*

Night Cap

2 oz. Old Mr. Boston Imported Rum
1 Teaspoon Powdered Sugar
Add enough warm milk to fill a Tom & Jerry Mug and stir. Grate a little nutmeg on top.

Ninitchka Cocktail

1½ oz. Old Mr. Boston Vodka
½ oz. Old Mr. Boston Creme de Cacao
½ oz. Lemon Juice
Shake well with cracked ice and strain into 3 oz. cocktail glass.

North Pole Cocktail

White of 1 Egg
½ oz. Lemon Juice
½ oz. Maraschino
1 oz. Old Mr. Boston Dry Gin
Shake well with cracked ice and strain into 4 oz. cocktail glass and top with whipped cream.

Old Fashioned Cocktail

Use Old Fashioned cocktail glass.
½ Lump of Sugar
2 Dashes Bitters
Add enough water to cover sugar and muddle well.
1 Cube of Ice
2 oz. Old Mr. Boston Whiskey*
Stir well. Add twist of lemon rind and drop in glass. Decorate with slice of orange, lemon and a cherry. Serve with stirring rod.

Old Pal Cocktail

½ oz. Grenadine
½ oz. Sweet Vermouth
1¼ oz. Old Mr. Boston Whiskey*
Stir well with cracked ice and strain into 3 oz. cocktail glass.

* *Bourbon, Blended, Rye or Canadian.*

O

Olympic Cocktail

¾ oz. Orange Juice
¾ oz. Curacao
¾ oz. Old Mr. Boston Five Star Brandy
Shake well with cracked ice and strain into 3 oz. cocktail glass.

Opal Cocktail

1 oz. Old Mr. Boston Dry Gin
½ oz. Orange Juice
½ oz. Triple Sec
¼ Teaspoon Powdered Sugar
½ Teaspoon Orange Flower Water
Shake well with cracked ice and strain into 3 oz. cocktail glass.

Opening Cocktail

½ oz. Grenadine
½ oz. Sweet Vermouth
1¼ oz. Old Mr. Boston Whiskey*
Stir well with cracked ice and strain into 3 oz. cocktail glass.

Opera Cocktail

½ oz. Maraschino
½ oz. Dubonnet
1½ oz. Old Mr. Boston Dry Gin
Stir well with cracked ice and strain into 3 oz. cocktail glass.

Orangeade

Juice 2 Oranges
1 Teaspoon Powdered Sugar
Add 2 cubes of ice and enough water to fill 12 oz. Tom Collins glass and stir well. Decorate with a slice of orange, lemon and 2 cherries. Serve with straws.

Orange Blossom Cocktail

1 oz. Old Mr. Boston Dry Gin
1 oz. Orange Juice
¼ Teaspoon Powdered Sugar
Shake well with cracked ice and strain into 3 oz. cocktail glass.

Orange Gin Collins

Juice ½ Lemon
2 oz. Old Mr. Boston Orange Flavored Gin
Shake well with cracked ice and strain into 12 oz. Tom Collins glass. Add several cubes of ice, fill with carbonated water and stir. Decorate with slice of lemon, orange and a cherry. Serve with straws.

Orange Gin Fizz

Juice ½ Lemon
1 Teaspoon Powdered Sugar
2 oz. Old Mr. Boston Orange Flavored Gin
Shake well with cracked ice and strain into 7 oz. highball glass. Fill with carbonated water and stir.

Orange Gin Highball

1 Cube of Ice
2 oz. Old Mr. Boston Orange Flavored Gin
Fill 8 oz. highball glass with ginger ale or carbonated water. Add twist of lemon peel, if desired, and stir.

---

* *Bourbon, Blended, Rye or Canadian.*

OLD
Mr.BOSTON
Fine Liquors
Boston Trade Mark
In Use Since 1868
MR. BOSTON'S
De Luxe
BLENDED WHISKEY
BLENDED AND BOTTLED BY
MR. BOSTON DISTILLER INC. BOSTON, MASS

P

Orange Gin Rickey

1 Cube of Ice
Juice ½ Lime
2 oz. Old Mr. Boston Orange Flavored Gin
Fill 8 oz. highball glass with carbonated water and stir. Leave lime in glass.

Orange Milk Fizz

Juice ½ Lemon
1 Teaspoon Powdered Sugar
2 oz. Old Mr. Boston Orange Flavored Gin
2 oz. Milk
Shake well with cracked ice and strain into 8 oz. highball glass. Fill with carbonated water and stir.

Orange Smile

1 Egg
Juice 1 Large Orange
1 Tablespoon Raspberry Syrup or Grenadine
Shake well with cracked ice and strain into 8 oz. stem goblet.

Orchid Cocktail

2 oz. Old Mr. Boston Dry Gin
1 Egg White
1 Dash of Creme de Yvette
Shake well with cracked ice and strain into 4 oz. cocktail glass.

Oriental Cocktail

1 oz. Old Mr. Boston Whiskey*
½ oz. Sweet Vermouth
½ oz. Curacao
Juice of ½ Lime
Shake well with cracked ice and strain into 3 oz. cocktail glass.

Paddy Cocktail

1¼ oz. Irish Whiskey
1¼ oz. Sweet Vermouth
1 Dash Bitters
Stir well with cracked ice and strain into 3 oz. cocktail glass.

Palm Beach Cocktail

1½ oz. Old Mr. Boston Dry Gin
¼ oz. Sweet Vermouth
¼ oz. Grapefruit Juice
Shake well with cracked ice and strain into 3 oz. cocktail glass.

* *Bourbon, Blended, Rye or Canadian.*

Deluxe Blended Whiskey 86 Proof 65% Grain Neutral Spirits

P

Palmer Cocktail
2 oz. Old Mr. Boston Whiskey*
1 Dash Bitters
½ Teaspoon Lemon Juice
Stir well with cracked ice and strain into 3 oz. cocktail glass.

Palmetto Cocktail
1¼ oz. Old Mr. Boston Imported Rum
1¼ oz. Dry Vermouth
2 Dashes Bitters
Stir well with cracked ice and strain into 3 oz. cocktail glass.

Panama Cocktail
1 oz. Old Mr. Boston Creme de Cacao
1 oz. Sweet Cream
1 oz. Old Mr. Boston Five Star Brandy
Shake well with cracked ice and strain into 4 oz. cocktail glass.

Paradise Cocktail
1 oz. Old Mr. Boston Apricot Flavored Brandy
¾ oz. Old Mr. Boston Dry Gin
Juice ¼ Orange
Shake well with cracked ice and strain into 3 oz. cocktail glass.

Parisian Blonde Cocktail
¾ oz. Sweet Cream
¾ oz. Curacao
¾ oz. Jamaica Rum
Shake well with cracked ice and strain into 3 oz. cocktail glass.

Passion Daiquiri Cocktail
1½ oz. Old Mr. Boston Imported Rum
Juice 1 Lime
1 Teaspoon Powdered Sugar
½ oz. Passion Fruit Juice
Shake well with cracked ice and strain into 3 oz. cocktail glass.

Peach Blossom
1 Teaspoon Lemon Juice
½ Teaspoon Powdered Sugar
2 oz. Old Mr. Boston Dry Gin
½ Peach
Shake well with cracked ice and strain into 8 oz. highball glass. Fill with carbonated water and stir.

Peach Blow Fizz
Juice ½ Lemon
White of 1 Egg
2 Teaspoons Grenadine
½ Teaspoon Powdered Sugar
1 oz. Sweet Cream
2 oz. Old Mr. Boston Dry Gin
Shake well with cracked ice and strain into 10 oz. highball glass. Fill with carbonated water and stir.

Peach Sangaree
2 oz. Old Mr. Boston Peach Flavored Brandy
2 cubes of Ice
Serve in 8 oz. highball glass. Fill balance with soda water. Stir, leaving enough room on which to float a tablespoon of Port Wine. Sprinkle lightly with nutmeg.

* *Bourbon, Blended, Rye or Canadian.*

P

PEGGY COCKTAIL
¾ oz. Dry Vermouth
1½ oz. Old Mr. Boston Dry Gin
¼ Teaspoon Absinthe Substitute
¼ Teaspoon Dubonnet
Stir well with cracked ice and strain into 3 oz. cocktail glass.

PENDENNIS TODDY
Muddle lump of sugar with 1 teaspoon of water, in 6 oz. sour glass. Fill with finely shaved ice, add 2 oz. Old Mr. Boston Whiskey* and stir. Decorate with 2 slices of lemon.

PERFECT COCKTAIL
¼ oz. Dry Vermouth
¼ oz. Sweet Vermouth
1½ oz. Old Mr. Boston Dry Gin
1 Dash Bitters
Stir well with cracked ice and strain into 3 oz. cocktail glass.

PETER PAN COCKTAIL
2 Dashes Bitters
¾ oz. Orange Juice
¾ oz. Dry Vermouth
¾ oz. Old Mr. Boston Dry Gin
Shake well with cracked ice and strain into 3 oz. cocktail glass.

PHOEBE SNOW COCKTAIL
1¼ oz. Dubonnet
1¼ oz. Old Mr. Boston Five Star Brandy
¼ Teaspoon Absinthe Substitute
Stir well with cracked ice and strain into 3 oz. cocktail glass.

PICCADILLY COCKTAIL
¾ oz. Dry Vermouth
1½ oz. Old Mr. Boston Dry Gin
¼ Teaspoon Absinthe Substitute
¼ Teaspoon Grenadine
Stir well with cracked ice and strain into 3 oz. cocktail glass.

PICON COCKTAIL
See **AMER PICON COCKTAIL** *on page 3.*

PIKE'S PEAK COOLER
Juice ½ Lemon
1 Teaspoon Powdered Sugar
1 Egg
Shake well with cracked ice and strain into 12 oz. Tom Collins glass and fill with hard cider and stir. Insert spiral of orange or lemon peel (or both) and dangle end over rim of glass.

PINEAPPLE COCKTAIL
¾ oz. Pineapple Juice
1½ oz. Old Mr. Boston Imported Rum
½ Teaspoon Lemon Juice
Shake well with cracked ice and strain into 3 oz. cocktail glass.

PINEAPPLE COOLER
Into 12 oz. Tom Collins glass, put:
2 oz. Pineapple Juice
½ Teaspoon Powdered Sugar
2 oz. Carbonated Water
Stir; fill glass with cracked ice and add: 2 oz. Dry White Wine. *Fill with carbonated water and stir again. Insert spiral of orange or lemon peel (or both) and dangle end over rim of glass.*

---

* *Bourbon, Blended, Rye or Canadian.*

P

Pineapple Fizz

1 oz. Pineapple Juice
½ Teaspoon Powdered Sugar
2 oz. Old Mr. Boston Imported Rum
Shake well with cracked ice and strain into 7 oz. highball glass. Fill with carbonated water and stir.

Ping-Pong Cocktail

Juice of ¼ Lemon
White of 1 Egg
1 oz. Old Mr. Boston Sloe Gin
1 oz. Creme de Yvette
Shake well with cracked ice and strain into 4 oz. cocktail glass.

Pink Pussy Cat

Use 7 oz. Highball glass almost filled with shaved ice and add:
1½ oz. Old Mr. Boston Vodka or Dry Gin
Fill balance of glass with pineapple or grapefruit juice. Add dash of Grenadine for color and stir.

Pink Gin

See Gin and Bitters *page 40.*

Pink Lady Cocktail

White of 1 Egg
1 Teaspoon Grenadine
1 Teaspoon Sweet Cream
1½ oz. Old Mr. Boston Dry Gin
Shake well with cracked ice and strain into 4 oz. cocktail glass.

Pink Rose Fizz

Juice ½ Lemon
1 Teaspoon Powdered Sugar
White of 1 Egg
½ Teaspoon Grenadine
2 Teaspoons Sweet Cream
2 oz. Old Mr. Boston Dry Gin
Shake well with cracked ice and strain into 8 oz. highball glass. Fill with carbonated water and stir.

Pink Squirrel Cocktail

1 oz. Creme de Almond Liqueur
½ oz. Old Mr. Boston Creme de Cacao (white)
½ oz. Light Cream
Shake well with cracked ice and strain into 3 oz. cocktail glass.

Plain Vermouth Cocktail

See Vermouth Cocktail *page 103.*

Planter's Cocktail

Juice of ¼ Lemon
½ Teaspoon Powdered Sugar
1½ oz. Jamaica Rum
Shake well with cracked ice and strain into 3 oz. cocktail glass.

Mr. BOSTON
VODKA
OLD
Mr. BOSTON
VODKA
80 PROOF – 4/5 QUART
PRODUCED AND BOTTLED BY

P

Planter's Punch No. 1
Juice 2 Limes
2 Teaspoons Powdered Sugar
2 oz. Carbonated Water
Fill 12 oz. Tom Collins glass with shaved ice and stir until glass is frosted. Add 2 dashes Bitters, 2½ oz. Old Mr. Boston Imported Rum. Stir and decorate with slice of lemon, orange, pineapple and a cherry. Serve with straws.

Planter's Punch No. 2
Juice 1 Lime
Juice ½ Lemon
Juice ½ Orange
1 Teaspoon Pineapple Juice
2 oz. Old Mr. Boston Imported Rum
Pour above into 16 oz. glass, well filled with shaved ice. Stir until glass is frosted. Then add 1 oz. Jamaica Rum, and top with ¼ teaspoon Curacao. Decorate with slice of orange, lemon, pineapple and a cherry, also sprig of mint dipped in powdered sugar. Serve with straws.

Plaza Cocktail
¾ oz. Sweet Vermouth
¾ oz. Dry Vermouth
¾ oz. Old Mr. Boston Dry Gin
1 Strip of Pineapple
Shake well with cracked ice and strain into 3 oz. cocktail glass.

Poker Cocktail
1¼ oz. Sweet Vermouth
1¼ oz. Old Mr. Boston Imported Rum
Stir well with cracked ice and strain into 3 oz. cocktail glass.

Pollyanna Cocktail
Muddle 3 slices of orange and 3 slices of pineapple
2 oz. Old Mr. Boston Dry Gin
½ oz. Sweet Vermouth
½ Teaspoon Grenadine
Shake well with cracked ice and strain into 4 oz. cocktail glass.

Polo Cocktail
½ oz. Lemon Juice
½ oz. Orange Juice
1 oz. Old Mr. Boston Dry Gin
Shake well with cracked ice and strain into 3 oz. cocktail glass.

Polynesian Cocktail
1½ oz. Old Mr. Boston Vodka
¾ oz. Old Mr. Boston Wild Cherry Flavored Brandy
Juice of 1 Lime
Shake well with cracked ice and strain into 4 oz. cocktail glass. Frost rim by rubbing with lime and dipping in powdered sugar.

Poop Deck Cocktail
1¼ oz. Old Mr. Boston Blackberry Flavored Brandy
½ oz. Port Wine
½ oz. Old Mr. Boston Five Star Brandy
Stir well with cracked ice and strain into 3 oz. cocktail glass.

Poppy Cocktail
¾ oz. Old Mr. Boston Creme de Cacao
1½ oz. Old Mr. Boston Dry Gin
Shake well with cracked ice and strain into 3 oz. cocktail glass.

P

PORT AND STARBOARD

½ oz. Grenadine
½ oz. Old Mr. Boston Creme de Menthe (green)
Pour carefully into Pousse Café glass, so that Menthe floats on Grenadine.

PORT MILK PUNCH

1 Teaspoon Powdered Sugar
3 oz. Port Wine
½ pt. Milk
Shake well with cracked ice, strain into 12 oz. Tom Collins glass and grate nutmeg on top.

PORT WINE COBBLER

Dissolve 1 teaspoon powdered sugar in 2 oz. carbonated water; then fill 10 oz. goblet with shaved ice and add 3 oz. Port Wine. Stir well and decorate with fruits in season. Serve with straws.

PORT WINE COCKTAIL

2¼ oz. Port Wine
½ Teaspoon Old Mr. Boston Five Star Brandy
Stir slightly with cracked ice and strain into 3 oz. cocktail glass.

PORT WINE EGGNOG

1 Egg
1 Teaspoon Powdered Sugar
3 oz. Port Wine
Fill glass with milk. Shake well with cracked ice and strain into 12 oz. Tom Collins glass. Grate nutmeg on top.

PORT WINE FLIP

1 Egg
1 Teaspoon Powdered Sugar
1½ oz. Port Wine
2 Teaspoons Sweet Cream (if desired)
Shake well with cracked ice and strain into 5 oz. flip glass. Grate a little nutmeg on top.

PORT WINE NEGUS

½ Lump Sugar
2 oz. Port Wine
Fill hot whiskey glass with hot water and stir. Grate nutmeg on top.

PORT WINE SANGAREE

Dissolve ½ teaspoon powdered sugar in 1 teaspoon of water.
2 oz. Port Wine
2 cubes of Ice
Serve in 8 oz. highball glass. Fill balance with soda water. Stir, leaving enough room on which to float a tablespoon of Brandy. Sprinkle lightly with nutmeg.

POUSSE CAFÉ

⅙ Grenadine
⅙ Yellow Chartreuse
⅙ Creme de Yvette
⅙ Old Mr. Boston Creme de Menthe (white)
⅙ Green Chartreuse
⅙ Old Mr. Boston Five Star Brandy
Pour carefully, in order given, into Pousse Café glass so that each ingredient floats on preceding one.

See Index on page 145 for complete list of Pousse Café *recipes.*

P

Pousse L'Amour

⅓ oz. Maraschino
Yolk of 1 Egg
⅓ oz. Benedictine
⅓ oz. Old Mr. Boston Five Star Brandy
Pour carefully, in order given, into 2 oz. Sherry glass, so that each ingredient floats on preceding one.

Prairie Hen Cocktail

1 Whole Egg
1 Teaspoon Worcestershire Sauce
½ Teaspoon Vinegar
1 Drop Tabasco Sauce
Season with a little salt and pepper. Use 5 oz. Delmonico glass.

Prairie Oyster Cocktail

1 Whole Egg
1 Teaspoon Worcestershire Sauce
1 Teaspoon Tomato Catsup
½ Teaspoon Vinegar
Pinch of Pepper
1 Drop Tabasco Sauce
Use 5 oz. Delmonico glass.

Preakness Cocktail

¾ oz. Sweet Vermouth
1½ oz. Old Mr. Boston Whiskey*
1 Dash Bitters
½ Teaspoon Benedictine
Stir well with cracked ice and strain into 3 oz. cocktail glass. Add twist of lemon peel and drop in glass.

Presto Cocktail

½ oz. Orange Juice
½ oz. Sweet Vermouth
1¼ oz. Old Mr. Boston Five Star Brandy
¼ Teaspoon Absinthe Substitute
Shake well with cracked ice and strain into 3 oz. cocktail glass.

Prince's Smile Cocktail

½ oz. Old Mr. Boston Apricot Flavored Brandy
½ oz. Apple Brandy
1 oz. Old Mr. Boston Dry Gin
¼ Teaspoon Lemon Juice
Shake well with cracked ice and strain into 3 oz. cocktail glass.

Princess Pousse Cafe

¾ oz. Old Mr. Boston Apricot Flavored Brandy
¼ oz. Sweet Cream
Pour cream carefully on top, so that it does not mix. Use Pousse Café glass.

Princeton Cocktail

1 oz. Old Mr. Boston Dry Gin
1 oz. Dry Vermouth
Juice ½ Lime
Stir well with cracked ice and strain into 3 oz. cocktail glass.

Punches

See Index on page 145 for complete list of Punch *recipes.*

* *Bourbon, Blended, Rye or Canadian.*

Quaker's Cocktail

¾ oz. Old Mr. Boston Imported Rum
¾ oz. Old Mr. Boston Five Star Brandy
Juice ¼ Lemon
2 Teaspoons Raspberry Syrup
Shake well with cracked ice and strain into 3 oz. cocktail glass.

Quarter Deck Cocktail

⅓ oz. Sherry Wine
1½ oz. Old Mr. Boston Imported Rum
Juice ½ Lime
Stir well with cracked ice and strain into 3 oz. cocktail glass.

Queen Charlotte

2 oz. Claret Wine
1 oz. Raspberry Syrup or Grenadine
Pour into 12 oz. Tom Collins glass. Add cub of ice; fill with lemon soda and stir.

Queen Elizabeth Cocktail

1½ oz. Old Mr. Boston Dry Gin
½ oz. Dry Vermouth
¼ oz. Benedictine
Stir well with cracked ice and strain into 3 oz. cocktail glass.

Racquet Club Cocktail

1½ oz. Old Mr. Boston Dry Gin
¾ oz. Dry Vermouth
1 Dash Orange Bitters
Stir well with cracked ice and strain into 3 oz. cocktail glass.

Ramos Fizz

Juice ½ Lemon
White of 1 Egg
1 Teaspoon Powdered Sugar
2 oz. Old Mr. Boston Dry Gin
1 Tablespoon Sweet Cream
½ Teaspoon Orange Flower Water
Shake well with cracked ice and strain into 12 oz. Tom Collins glass. Fill with carbonated water and stir.

Rattlesnake Cocktail

1½ oz. Old Mr. Boston Whiskey*
White of 1 Egg
1 Teaspoon Lemon Juice
½ Teaspoon Powdered Sugar
¼ Teaspoon Absinthe Substitute
Shake well with cracked ice and strain into 4 oz. cocktail glass.

Red Swizzle

Make same as Gin Swizzle *(see page 43), and add 1 tablespoon of grenadine. If desired, rum, brandy or whiskey may be substituted for the gin.*

Reform Cocktail

¾ oz. Dry Vermouth
1½ oz. Sherry Wine
1 Dash Orange Bitters
Stir well with cracked ice and strain into 3 oz. cocktail glass. Serve with a cherry.

Remsen Cooler

Into 12 oz. Tom Collins glass, put:
½ Teaspoon Powdered Sugar
2 oz. Carbonated Water
Stir; fill glass with Cracked Ice and add:
2 oz. Old Mr. Boston Dry Gin
Fill with carbonated water or ginger ale and stir again. Insert spiral of orange or lemon peel (or both) and dangle end over rim of glass.

* *Bourbon, Blended, Rye or Canadian.*

R

Resolute Cocktail

Juice ¼ Lemon
½ oz. Old Mr. Boston Apricot Flavored Brandy
1 oz. Old Mr. Boston Dry Gin
Shake well with cracked ice and strain into 3 oz. cocktail glass.

Rhine Wine Cup

Use Large Glass Pitcher
4 Teaspoons Powdered Sugar
6 oz. Carbonated Water
½ oz. Triple Sec
½ oz. Curacao
2 oz. Old Mr. Boston Five Star Brandy
Fill pitcher with cubes of ice. Add 1 pint of Rhine wine. Stir well and decorate with as many fruits as available and also rind of cucumber inserted on each side of pitcher. Top with small bunch of mint sprigs. Serve in 5 oz. Claret glass.

Rickies

See Index on page 145 for complete list of Rickey *recipes.*

Rob Roy Cocktail

¾ oz. Sweet Vermouth
1½ oz. Old Mr. Boston Scotch Whisky
1 Dash Orange Bitters
Stir well with cracked ice and strain into 3 oz. cocktail glass.

Robert E. Lee Cooler

Into 12 oz. Tom Collins glass, put:
Juice ½ Lime
½ Teaspoon Powdered Sugar
2 oz. Carbonated Water, and stir
Fill glass with cracked ice and add:
¼ Teaspoon Absinthe Substitute
2 oz. Old Mr. Boston Dry Gin
Fill with ginger ale and stir again. Insert spiral of orange or lemon peel (or both) and dangle end over rim of glass.

Robson Cocktail

2 Teaspoons Lemon Juice
½ oz. Orange Juice
¼ oz. Grenadine
1 oz. Jamaica Rum
Shake well with cracked ice and strain into 3 oz. cocktail glass.

Rock & Rye Cocktail

1 oz. Old Mr. Boston Rock & Rye
1 oz. White Port Wine
¼ oz. Dry Vermouth
Stir well with cracked ice and strain into 3 oz. cocktail glass.

Rolls-Royce Cocktail

½ oz. Dry Vermouth
½ oz. Sweet Vermouth
1¼ oz. Old Mr. Boston Dry Gin
¼ Teaspoon Benedictine
Stir well with cracked ice and strain into 3 oz. cocktail glass.

Roma Cocktail

1 oz. Old Mr. Boston Dry Gin
½ oz. Dry Vermouth
½ oz. Sweet Vermouth
Add 2 or 3 strawberries. Shake well with cracked ice and strain into 3 oz. cocktail glass.

R

Rory O'More

¾ oz. Sweet Vermouth
1½ oz. Irish Whiskey
1 Dash Orange Bitters
Stir well with cracked ice and strain into 3 oz. cocktail glass.

Rose Cocktail (English)

½ oz. Old Mr. Boston Apricot Flavored Brandy
½ oz. Dry Vermouth
1 oz. Old Mr. Boston Dry Gin
½ Teaspoon Lemon Juice
1 Teaspoon Grenadine
Shake well with cracked ice and strain into 3 oz. cocktail glass. Frost edge of glass by rubbing with lemon and dipping in powdered sugar.

Rose Cocktail (French)

½ oz. Old Mr. Boston Wild Cherry Flavored Brandy
½ oz. Dry Vermouth
1¼ oz. Old Mr. Boston Dry Gin
Stir well with cracked ice and strain into 3 oz. cocktail glass.

Roselyn Cocktail

¾ oz. Dry Vermouth
1½ oz. Old Mr. Boston Dry Gin
½ Teaspoon Grenadine
Stir well with cracked ice and strain into 3 oz. cocktail glass. Twist of lemon peel on top and drop in glass.

Royal Clover Club Cocktail

Juice 1 Lime
1 Tablespoon Grenadine
Yolk 1 Egg
1½ oz. Old Mr. Boston Dry Gin
Shake well with cracked ice and strain into 4 oz. cocktail glass.

Royal Cocktail

1 Whole Egg
Juice ½ Lemon
1 Teaspoon Powdered Sugar
1½ oz. Old Mr. Boston Dry Gin
Shake well with cracked ice and strain into 4 oz. cocktail glass.

Royal Fizz

Juice ½ Lemon
1 Teaspoon Powdered Sugar
2 oz. Old Mr. Boston Dry Gin
1 Whole Egg
Shake well with cracked ice and strain into 8 oz. highball glass. Fill with carbonated water and stir.

Royal Purple Punch

Pour 2 large bottles (⅘ quart size) Claret Wine and 2 large bottles ginger ale over ice cubes in punch bowl. Stir well. Float thin slices of lemon studded with cloves on top. Serve in 4 oz. punch glasses.

Royal Smile Cocktail

Juice ¼ Lemon
1 Teaspoon Grenadine
½ oz. Old Mr. Boston Dry Gin
1 oz. Apple Brandy
Stir well with cracked ice and strain into 3 oz. cocktail glass.

Ruby Fizz

Juice ½ Lemon
1 Teaspoon Powdered Sugar
White of 1 Egg
1 Teaspoon Grenadine
2 oz. Old Mr. Boston Sloe Gin
Shake well with cracked ice and strain into 8 oz. highball glass. Fill with carbonated water and stir.

KING'S MEN
IMPORTED
MR. BOSTON'S IMPORTED
KING'S MEN
Blended
SCOTCH
Whisky
100% SCOTCH WHISKIES
IMPORTED
IMPORTED FROM SCOTLAND
IMPORTED FROM SCOTLAND
Old Mr. Boston
PRODUCT OF SCOTLAND
BLENDED
SCOTCH
WHISKY
100% SCOTCH WHISKIES
IMPORTED
IMPORTED
DESMOND & DUFF
SCOTCH
PARTNERSHIP AGREEMENT
D&D

R

Rum Cobbler

Dissolve, in a 10 oz. goblet,
1 Teaspoon Powdered Sugar
2 oz. Carbonated Water
Fill goblet with shaved ice, and add:
2 oz. Old Mr. Boston Imported Rum
Stir well and decorate with fruits in season. Serve with straws.

Rum Cola

See Cuba Libra *Page 29.*

Rum Collins

Juice 1 Lime
1 Teaspoon Powdered Sugar
2 oz. Old Mr. Boston Imported Rum
Shake well with cracked ice and strain into 12 oz. Tom Collins glass. Add several cubes of ice, fill with carbonated water and stir. Decorate with slice of lemon and a cherry and drop lime in glass. Serve with straws.

Rum Cooler

Into 12 oz. Tom Collins glass, put:
½ Teaspoon Powdered Sugar
2 oz. Carbonated Water
Stir; fill glass with cracked ice and add:
2 oz. Old Mr. Boston Imported Rum
Fill with carbonated water or ginger ale and stir again. Insert spiral of orange or lemon peel (or both) and dangle end over rim of glass.

Rum Daisy

Juice of ½ Lemon
½ Teaspoon Powdered Sugar
1 Teaspoon Raspberry Syrup or Grenadine
2 oz. Old Mr. Boston Imported Rum
Shake well with cracked ice and strain into Stein or 8 oz. metal cup. Add cube of ice and decorate with fruit.

Rum Eggnog

1 Egg
1 Teaspoon Powdered Sugar
2 oz. Old Mr. Boston Imported Rum
Fill glass with milk. Shake well with cracked ice and strain into 12 oz. Tom Collins glass. Grate nutmeg on top.

Rum Fix

Juice ½ Lemon or 1 Lime
1 Teaspoon Powdered Sugar
1 Teaspoon Water and stir
Fill glass with Shaved Ice
2½ oz. Old Mr. Boston Imported Rum
Use 8 oz. highball glass. Stir well. Add slice of lemon. Serve with straws.

Rum Highball

1 Cube of Ice
2 oz. Old Mr. Boston Imported Rum
Fill 8 oz. highball glass with ginger ale or carbonated water. Add twist of lemon peel, if desired, and stir.

R

Rum Milk Punch

1 Teaspoon Powdered Sugar
2 oz. Old Mr. Boston Imported Rum
½ pt. Milk
Shake well with cracked ice, strain into 12 oz. Tom Collins glass and grate nutmeg on top.

Rum Rickey

1 Cube of Ice
Juice ½ Lime
1½ oz. Old Mr. Boston Imported Rum
Fill 8 oz. highball glass with carbonated water and stir. Leave lime in glass.

Rum Sour

Juice ½ Lemon
½ Teaspoon Powdered Sugar
2 oz. Old Mr. Boston Imported Rum
Shake well with cracked ice and strain into 6 oz. sour glass. Decorate with a half-slice of lemon and a cherry.

Rum Swizzle

Made same as Gin Swizzle *(see page 43), using* 2 oz. Old Mr. Boston Imported Rum.

Rum Toddy

Use Old Fashioned cocktail glass.
½ Teaspoon Powdered Sugar
2 Teaspoons Water
Stir.
2 oz. Old Mr. Boston Imported Rum
1 Lump of Ice
Stir again and twist lemon peel on top.

Rum Toddy (Hot)

Put lump of sugar into hot Whiskey glass and fill two-thirds with boiling water. Add 2 oz. Old Mr. Boston Imported Rum. *Stir and decorate with slice of lemon. Grate nutmeg on top.*

Russian Bear Cocktail

1 oz. Old Mr. Boston Vodka
½ oz. Old Mr. Boston Creme de Cacao
½ oz. Sweet Cream
Stir well with cracked ice and strain into 3 oz. cocktail glass.

Russian Cocktail

¾ oz. Old Mr. Boston Creme de Cacao
¾ oz. Old Mr. Boston Dry Gin
¾ oz. Old Mr. Boston Vodka
Shake well with cracked ice and strain into 3 oz. cocktail glass.

Rusty Nail

¾ oz. Old Mr. Boston Scotch Whiskey
¾ oz. Drambuie
Serve in Old Fashioned cocktail glass with cubes of ice.

Rye Highball

1 Cube of Ice
2 oz. Old Mr. Boston Rye Whiskey
Fill 8 oz. highball glass with ginger ale or carbonated water. Add twist of lemon peel, if desired, and stir.

Rye Whiskey Cocktail

1 Dash Bitters
1 Teaspoon Simple Syrup
2 oz. Old Mr. Boston Rye Whiskey
Stir well with cracked ice and strain into 3 oz. cocktail glass. Serve with a cherry.

St. Patrick's Day Cocktail

¾ oz. Old Mr. Boston Creme de Menthe (green)
¾ oz. Green Chartreuse
¾ oz. Irish Whiskey
1 Dash Bitters
Stir well with cracked ice and strain into 3 oz. cocktail glass.

Salty Dog

Fill 12 oz. Tom Collins glass almost full with shaved ice or ice cubes and add:
2 oz. Old Mr. Boston Dry Gin
2 oz. Grapefruit, Lemon or Lime Juice
¼ Teaspoon Salt
Stir well.

San Francisco Cocktail

¾ oz. Old Mr. Boston Sloe Gin
¾ oz. Sweet Vermouth
¾ oz. Dry Vermouth
1 Dash Bitters
1 Dash Orange Bitters
Shake well with cracked ice and strain into 3 oz. cocktail glass. Serve with a cherry.

Sand-Martin Cocktail

1 Teaspoon Green Chartreuse
1¼ oz. Sweet Vermouth
1¼ oz. Old Mr. Boston Dry Gin
Stir well with cracked ice and strain into 3 oz. cocktail glass.

Sangarees

See Index on page 146 for complete list of Sangaree *recipes.*

Santiago Cocktail

½ Teaspoon Powdered Sugar
¼ Teaspoon Grenadine
Juice 1 Lime
1½ oz. Old Mr. Boston Imported Rum
Shake well with cracked ice and strain into 3 oz. cocktail glass.

Saratoga Cocktail

2 oz. Old Mr. Boston Five Star Brandy
2 Dashes Bitters
½ Teaspoon Pineapple Syrup
½ Teaspoon Maraschino
Stir well with cracked ice and strain into 3 oz. cocktail glass.

Saratoga Cooler

Fill 12 oz. Tom Collins glass with cracked ice. Fill with sarsaparilla. Insert spiral of lemon and dangle end over rim of glass.

SAUCY SUE COCKTAIL

½ Teaspoon Old Mr. Boston
   Apricot Flavored Brandy
½ Teaspoon Absinthe Substitute
2 oz. Apple Brandy
Stir well with cracked ice and strain into 3 oz. cocktail glass.

SAUTERNE CUP

Use large glass pitcher.
4 Teaspoons Powdered Sugar
6 oz. Carbonated Water
½ oz. Triple Sec
½ oz. Curacao
2 oz. Old Mr. Boston Five Star Brandy
Fill pitcher with cubes of ice. Add 1 pint of Sauterne. Stir well and decorate with as many fruits as available and also rind of cucumber inserted on each side of pitcher. Top with small bunch of mint sprigs. Serve in 5 oz. Claret glass.

SAXON COCKTAIL

Juice ½ Lime
½ Teaspoon Grenadine
1¾ oz. Old Mr. Boston Imported Rum
1 Twist Orange Peel
Shake well with cracked ice and strain into 3 oz. cocktail glass.

SAZERAC COCKTAIL

Put ¼ Teaspoon Absinthe Substitute into an Old Fashioned cocktail glass and revolve glass until it is entirely coated with the Absinthe Substitute. Then add:
½ Lump of Sugar
2 Dashes Bitters
Sufficient water to cover sugar, and muddle well.
2 Cubes of Ice
2 oz. Old Mr. Boston Whiskey*
Stir very well. Add twist of lemon peel. (For best results, put glass on ice for a few minutes before using.)

SCOTCH BISHOP COCKTAIL

1 oz. Old Mr. Boston Scotch Whisky
½ oz. Orange Juice
½ oz. Dry Vermouth
½ Teaspoon Triple Sec
¼ Teaspoon Powdered Sugar
Twist of Lemon Peel
Shake well with cracked ice and strain into 3 oz. cocktail glass.

SCOTCH COOLER

2 oz. Old Mr. Boston Scotch Whisky
3 Dashes Old Mr. Boston Creme de Menthe (white)
Stir into 8 oz. highball glass with ice cubes. Fill with chilled carbonated water and stir.

SCOTCH MILK PUNCH

2 oz. Old Mr. Boston Scotch Whisky
6 oz. Milk
Teaspoon powdered sugar
Shake thoroughly with cracked ice. Pour into 12 oz. Tom Collins glass. Sprinkle with nutmeg.

---

* Bourbon, Blended, Rye or Canadian.

S

Scotch Mist
Fill Old Fashioned cocktail glass with shaved ice. Pour in Old Mr. Boston Scotch Whisky. Add twist of lemon peel. Serve with short straws.

Scotch Old Fashioned
Make same as Old Fashioned Cocktail *(See page 68), except substitute* Old Mr. Boston Scotch Whisky.

Scotch Rickey
1 Cube of Ice
Juice ½ Lime
1½ oz. Old Mr. Boston Scotch Whisky
Fill 8 oz. highball glass with carbonated water and stir. Leave lime in glass.

Scotch Sour
1½ oz. Old Mr. Boston Scotch Whisky
Juice of ½ Lime
½ Teaspoon Powdered Sugar
Shake well with cracked ice; strain into 6 oz. sour glass. Decorate with a half-slice of lemon and a cherry.

Scotch Stinger
Same as Stinger Cocktail on page 95, but substitute Old Mr. Boston Scotch Whiskey, *in place of Brandy.*

Scotch Whisky Highball
1 Cube of Ice
2 oz. Old Mr. Boston Scotch Whisky
Fill 8 oz. highball glass with ginger ale or carbonated water. Add twist of lemon peel, if desired, and stir.

Screwdriver
Put 2 or 3 cubes of ice into 6 oz. glass. Add 2 oz. Old Mr. Boston Vodka. Fill balance of glass with orange juice and stir.

Sensation Cocktail
Juice of ¼ Lemon
1½ oz. Old Mr. Boston Dry Gin
1 Teaspoon Maraschino
3 Sprigs Fresh Mint
Shake well with cracked ice and strain into 3 oz. cocktail glass.

September Morn Cocktail
White of 1 Egg
1½ oz. Old Mr. Boston Imported Rum
Juice of ½ Lime
1 Teaspoon Grenadine
Shake well with cracked ice and strain into 4 oz. cocktail glass.

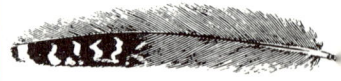

Seventh Heaven Cocktail
2 Teaspoons Grapefruit Juice
½ oz. Maraschino
1¼ oz. Old Mr. Boston Dry Gin
Shake well with cracked ice and strain into 3 oz. cocktail glass. Decorate with sprig of fresh mint.

Sevilla Cocktail
½ Teaspoon Powdered Sugar
1 Egg
1 oz. Port Wine
1 oz. Old Mr. Boston Imported Rum
Shake well with cracked ice and strain into 4 oz. cocktail glass.

S

SHAMROCK COCKTAIL

1½ oz. Irish Whiskey
½ oz. Dry Vermouth
1 Teaspoon Old Mr. Boston Creme de Menthe (green)
Stir well with cracked ice and strain into 3 oz. cocktail glass. Serve with an olive.

SHANDY GAFF

5 oz. Beer
5 oz. Ginger Ale
Use 12 oz. Tom Collins glass and stir very gently.

SHANGHAI COCKTAIL

Juice ¼ Lemon
1 Teaspoon Old Mr. Boston Anisette
1 oz. Jamaica Rum
½ Teaspoon Grenadine
Shake well with cracked ice and strain into 3 oz. cocktail glass.

SHERRY AND EGG COCKTAIL

Place an egg in a glass, being careful not to break the yolk. Fill glass with Sherry. Use 4 oz. cocktail glass.

SHERRY COBBLER

Dissolve:
1 Teaspoon Powdered Sugar
2 oz. Carbonated Water
Fill goblet with shaved ice; add:
3 oz. Sherry Wine
Stir well and decorate with fruits in season. Serve with straws.

SHERRY COCKTAIL

2½ oz. Sherry Wine
1 Dash Bitters
Stir well with cracked ice and strain into 3 oz. cocktail glass. Twist of orange peel and drop in glass.

SHERRY EGGNOG

1 Egg
1 Teaspoon Powdered Sugar
3 oz. Sherry Wine
Fill glass with milk. Shake well with cracked ice and strain into 12 oz. Tom Collins glass. Grate nutmeg on top.

SHERRY FLIP

1 Egg
1 Teaspoon Powdered Sugar
1½ oz. Sherry Wine
2 Teaspoons Sweet Cream (if desired)
Shake well with cracked ice and strain into 5 oz. flip glass. Grate a little nutmeg on top.

SHERRY MILK PUNCH

1 Teaspoon Powdered Sugar
3 oz. Sherry Wine
½ pt. Milk
Shake well with cracked ice, strain into 12 oz. Tom Collins glass and grate nutmeg on top.

S

Sherry Sangaree

Dissolve ½ teaspoon powdered sugar in 1 teaspoon of water. Add:
2 oz. Sherry Wine
2 cubes of Ice
Serve in 8 oz. highball glass. Fill balance with soda water. Stir, leaving enough room on which to float a tablespoon of Port Wine. Sprinkle lightly with nutmeg.

Sherry Twist Cocktail

1 oz. Sherry Wine
⅓ oz. Old Mr. Boston Five Star Brandy
⅓ oz. Dry Vermouth
⅓ oz. Triple Sec
½ Teaspoon Lemon Juice
Shake well with cracked ice and strain into 3 oz. cocktail glass. Top with pinch of cinnamon and twist of orange peel dropped in glass.

Shriner Cocktail

1¼ oz. Old Mr. Boston Five Star Brandy
1¼ oz. Old Mr. Boston Sloe Gin
2 Dashes Bitters
½ Teaspoon Simple Syrup
Stir well with cracked ice and strain into 3 oz. cocktail glass. Twist of lemon peel and drop into glass.

Sidecar Cocktail

Juice ¼ Lemon
½ oz. Triple Sec
1 oz. Old Mr. Boston Five Star Brandy
Shake well with cracked ice and strain into 3 oz. cocktail glass.

Silver Cocktail

1 oz. Dry Vermouth
1 oz. Old Mr. Boston Dry Gin
2 Dashes Orange Bitters
¼ Teaspoon Simple Syrup
½ Teaspoon Maraschino
Stir well with cracked ice and strain into 3 oz. cocktail glass. Twist of lemon peel and drop into glass.

Silver Fizz

Juice ½ Lemon
1 Teaspoon Powdered Sugar
2 oz. Old Mr. Boston Dry Gin
White of 1 Egg
Shake well with cracked ice and strain into 8 oz. highball glass. Fill with carbonated water and stir.

Silver King Cocktail

White of 1 Egg
Juice ¼ Lemon
1½ oz. Old Mr. Boston Dry Gin
½ Teaspoon Powdered Sugar
2 Dashes Orange Bitters
Shake well with cracked ice and strain into 4 oz. cocktail glass.

Silver Stallion Fizz

1 Scoop Vanilla Ice Cream
2 oz. Old Mr. Boston Dry Gin
Use 8 oz. highball glass; fill with carbonated water and stir.

S

Singapore Sling

Juice ½ Lemon
1 Teaspoon Powdered Sugar
2 oz. Old Mr. Boston Dry Gin
½ oz. Old Mr. Boston Wild Cherry Flavored Brandy
Shake well with cracked ice and strain into 12 oz. Tom Collins glass. Add ice cubes and fill with carbonated water; stir. Decorate with fruits in season and serve with straws.

Sir Walter Cocktail

¾ oz. Old Mr. Boston Imported Rum
¾ oz. Old Mr. Boston Five Star Brandy
1 Teaspoon Grenadine
1 Teaspoon Curacao
1 Teaspoon Lemon Juice
Shake well with cracked ice and strain into 3 oz. cocktail glass.

Slings

See Index on page 146 for complete list of Sling *recipes.*

Sloe Driver

Put 2 or 3 cubes of ice into 6 oz. glass and add:
2 oz. Old Mr. Boston Sloe Gin
Fill with orange juice and stir.

Sloe Gin Cocktail

2 oz. Old Mr. Boston Sloe Gin
1 Dash Orange Bitters
¼ Teaspoon Dry Vermouth
Stir well with cracked ice and strain into 3 oz. cocktail glass.

Sloe Gin Collins

Juice ½ Lemon
2 oz. Old Mr. Boston Sloe Gin
Shake well with cracked ice and strain into 12 oz. Tom Collins glass. Add several cubes of ice, fill with carbonated water and stir. Decorate with slice of lemon, orange and a cherry. Serve with straws.

Sloe Gin Fizz

Juice of ½ Lemon
1 Teaspoon Powdered Sugar
2 oz. Old Mr. Boston Sloe Gin
Shake well with cracked ice and strain into 8 oz. highball glass. Fill with carbonated water and stir. Decorate with slice of lemon.

Sloe Gin Flip

1 Egg
1 Teaspoon Powdered Sugar
½ oz. Old Mr. Boston Sloe Gin
2 Teaspoons Sweet Cream (if desired)
Shake well with cracked ice and strain into 5 oz. flip glass. Grate a little nutmeg on top.

Sloe Gin Rickey

1 Cube of Ice
Juice of ½ Lime
2 oz. Old Mr. Boston Sloe Gin
Fill 8 oz. highball glass with carbonated water and stir. Leave Lime in glass.

Sloeberry Cocktail

1 Dash Bitters
2 oz. Old Mr. Boston Sloe Gin
Stir well with cracked ice and strain into 3 oz. cocktail glass.

S

Sloppy Joe's Cocktail No. 1

Juice 1 Lime
¼ Teaspoon Curacao
¼ Teaspoon Grenadine
¾ oz. Old Mr. Boston Imported Rum
¾ oz. Dry Vermouth
Shake well with cracked ice and strain into 3 oz. cocktail glass.

Sloppy Joe's Cocktail No. 2

¾ oz. Pineapple Juice
¾ oz. Old Mr. Boston Five Star Brandy
¾ oz. Port Wine
¼ Teaspoon Curacao
¼ Teaspoon Grenadine
Shake well with cracked ice and strain into 3 oz. cocktail glass.

Smashes

See Index on page 146 for complete list of Smash *recipes.*

Smile Cocktail

1 oz. Grenadine
1 oz. Old Mr. Boston Dry Gin
½ Teaspoon Lemon Juice
Shake well with cracked ice and strain into 3 oz. cocktail glass.

Smiler Cocktail

½ oz. Sweet Vermouth
½ oz. Dry Vermouth
1 oz. Old Mr. Boston Dry Gin
1 Dash Bitters
¼ Teaspoon Orange Juice
Shake well with cracked ice and strain into 3 oz. cocktail glass.

Snowball Cocktail

1½ oz. Old Mr. Boston Dry Gin
½ oz. Old Mr. Boston Anisette
½ oz. Sweet Cream
Shake well with cracked ice and strain into 4 oz. cocktail glass.

Society Cocktail

1½ oz. Old Mr. Boston Dry Gin
¾ oz. Dry Vermouth
¼ Teaspoon Grenadine
Stir well with cracked ice and strain into 3 oz. cocktail glass.

Soother Cocktail

½ oz. Old Mr. Boston Five Star Brandy
½ oz. Apple Brandy
½ oz. Curacao
Juice ½ Lemon
1 Teaspoon Powdered Sugar
Shake well with cracked ice and strain into 3 oz. cocktail glass.

Soul Kiss Cocktail

¼ oz. Orange Juice
¼ oz. Dubonnet
¾ oz. Dry Vermouth
¾ oz. Old Mr. Boston Whiskey*
Shake well with cracked ice and strain into 3 oz. cocktail glass.

Sours

See Index on page 146 for complete list of Sour *recipes.*

Sourteq

See Tequila Sour *on page 97.*

* *Bourbon, Blended, Rye or Canadian.*

S

South Side Cocktail

Juice ½ Lemon
1 Teaspoon Powdered Sugar
2 Sprigs Fresh Mint
1½ oz. Old Mr. Boston Dry Gin
Shake well with cracked ice and strain into 3 oz. cocktail glass.

South Side Fizz

Juice ½ Lemon
1 Teaspoon Powdered Sugar
2 oz. Old Mr. Boston Dry Gin
Shake well with cracked ice and strain into 7 oz. highball glass. Fill with carbonated water and stir. Add fresh mint leaves.

Southern Gin Cocktail

2 oz. Old Mr. Boston Dry Gin
2 Dashes Orange Bitters
½ Teaspoon Curacao
Stir well with cracked ice and strain into 3 oz. cocktail glass. Twist of lemon peel and drop into glass.

Spanish Town Cocktail

2 oz. Old Mr. Boston Imported Rum
1 Teaspoon Curacao
Stir well with cracked ice and strain into 3 oz. cocktail glass.

Special Rough Cocktail

1¼ oz. Apple Brandy
1¼ oz. Old Mr. Boston Five Star Brandy
¼ Teaspoon Absinthe Substitute
Stir well with cracked ice and strain into 3 oz. cocktail glass.

Spencer Cocktail

¾ oz. Old Mr. Boston Apricot Flavored Brandy
1½ oz. Old Mr. Boston Dry Gin
1 Dash Bitters
¼ Teaspoon Orange Juice
Shake well with cracked ice and strain into 3 oz. cocktail glass. Add a cherry and twist of orange peel.

Sphinx Cocktail

1½ oz. Old Mr. Boston Dry Gin
¼ oz. Sweet Vermouth
¼ oz. Dry Vermouth
Stir well with cracked ice and strain into 3 oz. cocktail glass. Serve with slice of lemon on top.

Spring Feeling Cocktail

½ oz. Lemon Juice
½ oz. Green Chartreuse
1 oz. Old Mr. Boston Dry Gin
Shake well with cracked ice and strain into 3 oz. cocktail glass.

Spritzer Highball

Pour 3 oz. chilled Rhine Wine or Sauterne into 8 oz. highball glass with ice cubes. Fill balance with carbonated water and stir gently.

Stanley Cocktail

Juice ¼ Lemon
1 Teaspoon Grenadine
¾ oz. Old Mr. Boston Dry Gin
¾ oz. Old Mr. Boston Imported Rum
Shake well with cracked ice and strain into 3 oz. cocktail glass.

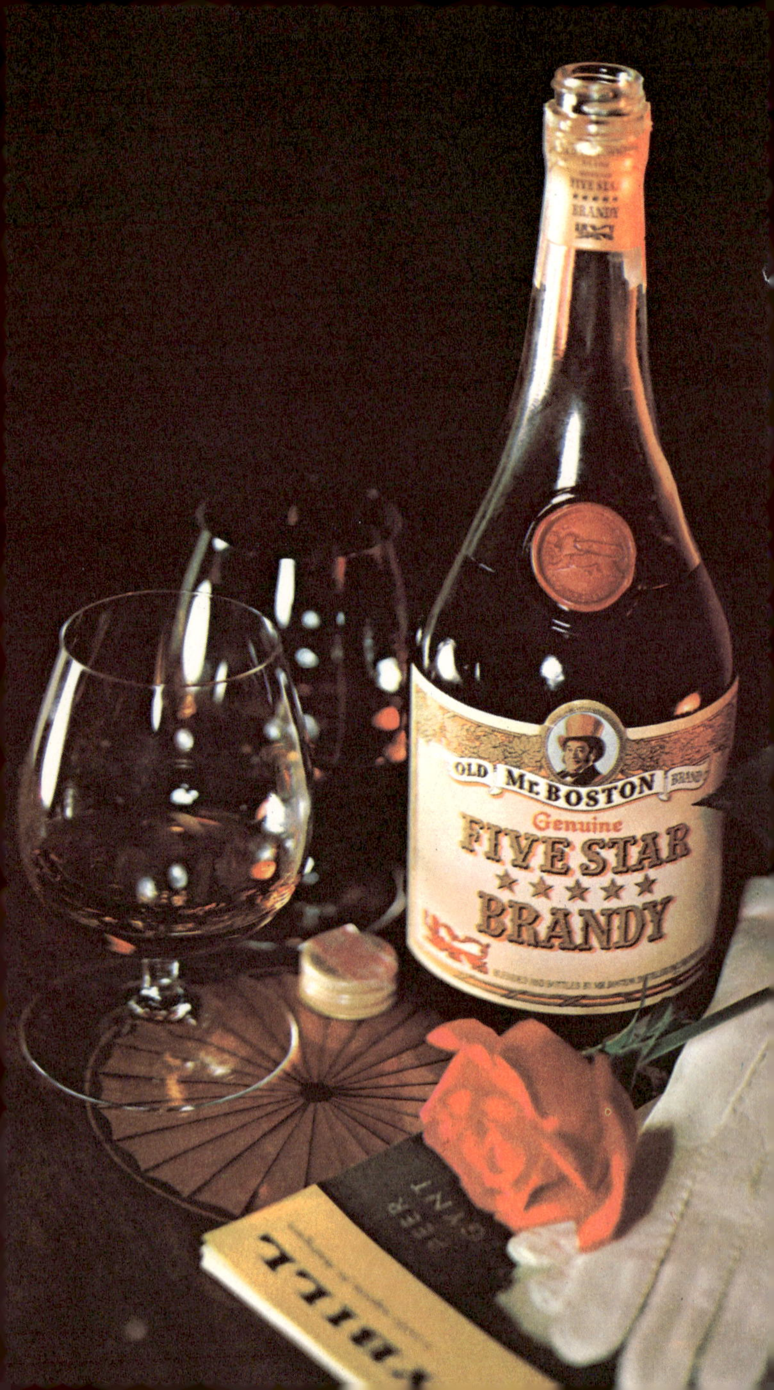

OLD Mr. BOSTON BRAND
Genuine
FIVE STAR
BRANDY

Star Cocktail

1 oz. Apple Brandy
1 oz. Sweet Vermouth
1 Dash Bitters
Stir well with cracked ice and strain into 3 oz. cocktail glass. Twist of lemon peel and drop into glass.

Star Daisy

Juice ½ Lemon
½ Teaspoon Powdered Sugar
1 Teaspoon Raspberry Syrup or Grenadine
1 oz. Old Mr. Boston Dry Gin
1 oz. Apple Brandy
Shake well with cracked ice and strain into stein or 8 oz. metal cup. Add cube of ice and decorate with fruit.

Stars and Stripes

⅓ Grenadine
⅓ Heavy Sweet Cream
⅓ Creme de Yvette
Pour carefully, in order given, into Pousse Café glass, so that each ingredient floats on preceding one.

Stinger Cocktail

1 oz. Old Mr. Boston Creme de Menthe (white)
1 oz. Old Mr. Boston Five Star Brandy
Shake well with cracked ice and strain into 3 oz. cocktail glass.

Stone Cocktail

½ oz. Old Mr. Boston Imported Rum
½ oz. Sweet Vermouth
1 oz. Sherry Wine
Stir well with cracked ice and strain into 3 oz. cocktail glass.

Stone Fence

1 Cube of Ice
2 Dashes Bitters
2 oz. Old Mr. Boston Scotch Whisky
Use 8 oz. highball glass and fill with carbonated water or cider and stir.

Straight Law Cocktail

¾ oz. Old Mr. Boston Dry Gin
1½ oz. Sherry Wine
Stir well with cracked ice and strain into 3 oz. cocktail glass.

Suissesse Cocktail

1½ oz. Absinthe Substitute
½ oz. Old Mr. Boston Anisette
White of 1 Egg
Shake well with cracked ice and strain into 4 oz. cocktail glass.

Sunshine Cocktail

¾ oz. Sweet Vermouth
1½ oz. Old Mr. Boston Dry Gin
1 Dash Bitters
Stir well with cracked ice and strain into 3 oz. cocktail glass. Twist of orange peel and drop into glass.

Susie Taylor

Juice ½ Lime
2 Cubes of Ice
2 oz. Old Mr. Boston Imported Rum
Fill 12 oz. Tom Collins glass with ginger ale and stir gently.

◀ Old Mr. Boston Five Star Brandy 80 and 84 Proof

Sweet Patootie Cocktail

1 oz. Old Mr. Boston Dry Gin
½ oz. Cointreau
½ oz. Orange Juice
Shake well with cracked ice and strain into 3 oz. cocktail glass.

Swiss Family Cocktail

½ Teaspoon Absinthe Substitute
2 Dashes Bitters
¾ oz. Dry Vermouth
1½ oz. Old Mr. Boston Whiskey*
Stir well with cracked ice and strain into 3 oz. cocktail glass.

Swizzles

See Index on page 147 for complete list of Swizzle *recipes.*

Tailspin Cocktail

¾ oz. Old Mr. Boston Dry Gin
¾ oz. Sweet Vermouth
¾ oz. Green Chartreuse
1 Dash Orange Bitters
Stir well with cracked ice and strain into 3 oz. cocktail glass. Twist of lemon peel and serve with cherry or olive.

Tango Cocktail

½ oz. Orange Juice
½ oz. Dry Vermouth
½ oz. Sweet Vermouth
1 oz. Old Mr. Boston Dry Gin
½ Teaspoon Curacao
Shake well with cracked ice and strain into 4 oz. cocktail glass.

Temptation Cocktail

1½ oz. Old Mr. Boston Whiskey*
½ Teaspoon Curacao
½ Teaspoon Absinthe Substitute
½ Teaspoon Dubonnet
1 Twist Orange Peel
1 Twist Lemon Peel
Shake well with cracked ice and strain into 3 oz. cocktail glass.

Tempter Cocktail

1 oz. Port Wine
1 oz. Old Mr. Boston Apricot Flavored Brandy
Stir well with cracked ice and strain into 3 oz. cocktail glass.

* *Bourbon, Blended, Rye or Canadian.*

T

Tequila Collins

Same as Tom Collins *(see page 100)* except use *Tequila instead of Dry Gin.*

Tequila Sour

Juice ½ Lemon
Teaspoon Powdered Sugar
2 oz. Tequila
Shake well with cracked ice and strain into 6 oz. sour glass. Decorate with a half-slice of lemon and a cherry.

Tequila Straight

½ Lemon
Pinch of Salt
Jigger Tequila
First suck lemon, place salt on tongue, then swallow Tequila.

Tequini Cocktail

1½ oz. Tequila
½ oz. Dry Vermouth
1 Dash Bitters may be added
Stir well with cracked ice and strain into 3 oz. cocktail glass. Serve with twist of lemon peel and an olive.

Tequonic

2 oz. Tequila
Juice of ½ Lemon or Lime
Pour Tequila over ice cubes in Old Fashioned cocktail glass. Add fruit juice; fill with tonic water and stir.

Thanksgiving Special Cocktail

¾ oz. Old Mr. Boston Apricot Flavored Brandy
¾ oz. Old Mr. Boston Dry Gin
¾ oz. Dry Vermouth
¼ Teaspoon Lemon Juice
Shake well with cracked ice and strain into 3 oz. cocktail glass. Serve with a cherry.

Third Degree Cocktail

1½ oz. Old Mr. Boston Dry Gin
¾ oz. Dry Vermouth
1 Teaspoon Absinthe Substitute
Stir well with cracked ice and strain into 3 oz. cocktail glass.

Third Rail Cocktail

¾ oz. Old Mr. Boston Imported Rum
¾ oz. Apple Brandy
¾ oz. Old Mr. Boston Five Star Brandy
¼ Teaspoon Absinthe Substitute
Stir well with cracked ice and strain into 3 oz. cocktail glass.

Thistle Cocktail

1¼ oz. Sweet Vermouth
1¼ oz. Old Mr. Boston Scotch Whisky
2 Dashes Bitters
Stir well with cracked ice and strain into 3 oz. cocktail glass.

OLD
Mr.BOSTON
Fine
Liquors
A TRUE FRUIT PRODUCT
BLACKBERRY
OLD Mr. BOSTON
BLACKBERRY
FLAVORED
BRANDY
PRODUCED AND BOTTLED BY
MR. BOSTON DISTILLER INC., BOSTON, MASS.
PRODUCED AND BOTTLED BY
MR. BOSTON DISTILLER INC.
BOSTON, MASS.

THREE MILLER COCKTAIL

1¼ oz. Old Mr. Boston Imported Rum
¾ oz. Old Mr. Boston Five Star Brandy
1 Teaspoon Grenadine
¼ Teaspoon Lemon Juice
Shake well with cracked ice and strain into 3 oz. cocktail glass.

THREE STRIPES COCKTAIL

1 oz. Old Mr. Boston Dry Gin
½ oz. Dry Vermouth
½ oz. Orange Juice
Shake well with cracked ice and strain into 3 oz. cocktail glass.

THUNDER COCKTAIL

1 Teaspoon Powdered Sugar
Yolk of 1 Egg
1½ oz. Old Mr. Boston Five Star Brandy
1 Pinch of Cayenne Pepper
Shake well with cracked ice and strain into 4 oz. cocktail glass.

THUNDER AND LIGHTNING COCKTAIL

Yolk of 1 Egg
1 Teaspoon Powdered Sugar
1½ oz. Old Mr. Boston Five Star Brandy
Shake well with cracked ice and strain into 4 oz. cocktail glass.

THUNDERCLAP COCKTAIL

¾ oz. Old Mr. Boston Dry Gin
¾ oz. Old Mr. Boston Whiskey*
¾ oz. Old Mr. Boston Five Star Brandy
Stir well with cracked ice and strain into 3 oz. cocktail glass.

* *Bourbon, Blended, Rye or Canadian.*

Ginger Flavored Brandy 70 Proof ▶
Flavored Brandy (Blackberry, Peach, Apricot and Cherry) 70 Proof

T

Tipperary Cocktail

¾ oz. Irish Whiskey
¾ oz. Green Chartreuse
¾ oz. Sweet Vermouth
Stir well with cracked ice and strain into 3 oz. cocktail glass.

T. N. T. Cocktail

1¼ oz. Old Mr. Boston Whiskey*
1¼ oz. Absinthe Substitute
Stir well with cracked ice and strain into 3 oz. cocktail glass.

Toddies

See Index on page 147 for complete list of Toddy *recipes.*

Tom and Jerry

First prepare batter, using mixing bowl. Separate the yolk and white of 1 egg, beating each separately and thoroughly. Then combine both, adding enough superfine powdered sugar to stiffen. Add to this 1 pinch of baking soda and ¼ oz. Old Mr. Boston Imported Rum to preserve the batter. Then add a little more sugar to stiffen. To serve, use hot Tom and Jerry mug, using 1 tablespoon of above batter, dissolved in 3 tablespoons hot milk. Add 1½ oz. Old Mr. Boston Imported Rum. Then fill mug with hot milk within ¼ inch of top of mug and stir gently. Then top with ½ oz. Old Mr. Boston Five Star Brandy and grate a little nutmeg on top.

The secret of a Tom and Jerry is to have a stiff batter and a warm mug.

Tom Collins

Juice of ½ Lemon
1 Teaspoon Powdered Sugar
2 oz. Old Mr. Boston Dry Gin
Shake well with cracked ice and strain into 12 oz. Tom Collins glass. Add several cubes of ice, fill with carbonated water and stir. Decorate with slice of lemon, orange and a cherry. Serve with straws.

Tovarich Cocktail

1½ oz. Old Mr. Boston Vodka
¾ oz. Old Mr. Boston Kummel
Juice of ½ Lime
Shake well with cracked ice and strain into 3 oz. cocktail glass.

Trilby Cocktail

1½ oz. Old Mr. Boston Whiskey*
¾ oz. Sweet Vermouth
2 Dashes Orange Bitters
Stir well with cracked ice and strain into 3 oz. cocktail glass.

Trinity Cocktail

¾ oz. Sweet Vermouth
¾ oz. Dry Vermouth
¾ oz. Old Mr. Boston Dry Gin
Stir well with cracked ice and strain into 3 oz. cocktail glass.

Tropical Cocktail

¾ oz. Old Mr. Boston Creme de Cacao
¾ oz. Maraschino
¾ oz. Dry Vermouth
1 Dash Bitters
Stir well with cracked ice and strain into 3 oz. cocktail glass.

* *Bourbon, Blended, Rye or Canadian.*

U

Tulip Cocktail

¼ oz. Lemon Juice
¼ oz. Old Mr. Boston Apricot Flavored Brandy
¾ oz. Sweet Vermouth
¾ oz. Apple Brandy
Shake well with cracked ice and strain into 3 oz. cocktail glass.

Turf Cocktail

¼ Teaspoon Absinthe Substitute
2 Dashes Bitters
1 oz. Dry Vermouth
1 oz. Old Mr. Boston Dry Gin
Stir well with cracked ice and strain into 3 oz. cocktail glass. Twist of orange peel and drop in glass.

Tuxedo Cocktail

1¼ oz. Old Mr. Boston Dry Gin
1¼ oz. Dry Vermouth
¼ Teaspoon Maraschino
¼ Teaspoon Absinthe Substitute
2 Dashes Orange Bitters
Stir well with cracked ice and strain into 3 oz. cocktail glass. Serve with a cherry.

Twin Six Cocktail

1 oz. Old Mr. Boston Dry Gin
½ oz. Sweet Vermouth
¼ Teaspoon Grenadine
½ oz. Orange Juice
White of 1 Egg
Shake well with cracked ice and strain into 4 oz. cocktail glass.

Twister

2 oz. Old Mr. Boston Vodka
Juice of ⅓ Lime
Pour into 12 oz. Tom Collins glass. Add several cubes of ice, drop rind into glass. Fill with Seven-Up and stir well.

Ulanda Cocktail

1½ oz. Old Mr. Boston Dry Gin
¾ oz. Triple Sec
¼ Teaspoon Absinthe Substitute
Stir well with cracked ice and strain into 3 oz. cocktail glass.

Union Jack Cocktail

¾ oz. Creme de Yvette
1½ oz. Old Mr. Boston Dry Gin
½ Teaspoon Grenadine
Shake well with cracked ice and strain into 3 oz. cocktail glass.

Old Mr. BOSTON
CREME de
CACAO
CONNOISSEUR
Old Mr. BOSTON
OLD
Mr. BOSTON
kümmel
CONNOISSEUR
Old Mr. BOSTON
Anisette

V

Valencia Cocktail

½ oz. Orange Juice
1½ oz. Old Mr. Boston Apricot Flavored Brandy
2 Dashes Orange Bitters
Shake well with cracked ice and strain into 3 oz. cocktail glass.

Vanderbilt Cocktail

¾ oz. Old Mr. Boston Wild Cherry Flavored Brandy
1½ oz. Old Mr. Boston Five Star Brandy
1 Teaspoon Simple Syrup
2 Dashes Bitters
Stir well with cracked ice and strain into 3 oz. cocktail glass.

Vermouth Cassis

¾ oz. Creme de Cassis
1½ oz. Dry Vermouth
1 Cube of Ice
Fill 8 oz. highball glass with carbonated water and stir.

Vermouth Cocktail

1 oz. Dry Vermouth
1 oz. Sweet Vermouth
1 Dash Orange Bitters
Stir well with cracked ice and strain into 3 oz. cocktail glass. Serve with a cherry.

Violet Fizz

Juice ½ Lemon
½ Teaspoon Powdered Sugar
1½ oz. Old Mr. Boston Dry Gin
½ oz. Creme de Yvette
Shake well with cracked ice and strain into 7 oz. highball glass. Fill with carbonated water and stir.

Vodka and Apple Juice

Put 2 or 3 cubes of ice into 6 oz. glass. Add 2 oz. Old Mr. Boston Vodka. Fill balance of glass with apple juice and stir.

Vodka and Tonic

2 oz. Old Mr. Boston Vodka
Cube of Ice
Use 12 oz. Tom Collins glass and fill balance with quinine tonic and stir.

Vodka Bloody Mary Cocktail

See Bloody Mary Cocktail on page 10.

Vodka Collins

Same as Tom Collins *(see page 100) except use* Old Mr. Boston Vodka *instead of dry gin.*

◀ (Cordials) Creme de Cacao 54 Proof White and Brown
Creme de Menthe 60 Proof White and Green
Kummel 70 Proof
Anisette 60 Proof

V

Vodka Cooler
Same as Gin Cooler *(see page 40), except use* Old Mr. Boston Vodka *instead of gin.*

Vodka Daisy
Juice ½ Lemon
½ Teaspoon Powdered Sugar
1 Teaspoon Grenadine
2 oz. Old Mr. Boston Vodka
Shake well with cracked ice and strain into stein or 8 oz. metal cup. Add cube of ice and decorate with fruit.

Vodka Gibson Cocktail
See Gibson Cocktail *on page 117.*

Vodka Gimlet Cocktail
Same as Gimlet Cocktail *(see page 40), except use* Old Mr. Boston Vodka *instead of gin.*

Vodka Grasshopper Cocktail
¾ oz. Old Mr. Boston Vodka
¾ oz. Old Mr. Boston Creme de Menthe (green)
¾ oz. Old Mr. Boston Creme de Cacao (white)
Shake well with cracked ice, strain into 3 oz. cocktail glass.

Vodka Gypsy Cocktail
1½ oz. Old Mr. Boston Vodka
¾ oz. Benedictine
1 Dash Bitters
Stir well with cracked ice and strain into 3 oz. cocktail glass.

Vodka Martini Cocktail
See *Special Martini Section* on pages 116 and 117.

Vodka on the Rocks
Put 2 or 3 ice cubes in Old Fashioned glass and add 2 oz. Old Mr. Boston Vodka. *Serve with a twist of lemon peel.*

Vodka "7"
2 oz. Old Mr. Boston Vodka
Juice ½ Lime
Use 12 oz. Tom Collins glass with cubes of ice. Drop lime in glass, fill balance with 7-Up and stir.

Vodka Sling
Same as Gin Sling *(See page 42), except use* Old Mr. Boston Vodka *instead of gin.*

Vodka Sour
Juice ½ Lemon
½ Teaspoon Powdered Sugar
2 oz. Old Mr. Boston Vodka
Shake well with cracked ice and strain into 6 oz. sour glass. Decorate with half-slice of lemon and a cherry.

Vodka Stinger
1 oz. Old Mr. Boston Vodka
1 oz. Old Mr. Boston Creme de Menthe (white)
Shake well with cracked ice and strain into 3 oz. cocktail glass.

Vodkatini
Same as Vodka Martini.

Wallick Cocktail

1¼ oz. Dry Vermouth
1¼ oz. Old Mr. Boston Dry Gin
1 Teaspoon Curacao
Stir well with cracked ice and strain into 3 oz. cocktail glass.

Ward Eight

Juice ½ Lemon
1 Teaspoon Powdered Sugar
1 Teaspoon Grenadine
2 oz. Old Mr. Boston Whiskey*
Shake well with cracked ice and strain into 8 oz. stem glass previously prepared with 2 cubes of ice, slice of orange, lemon and a cherry. Serve with straws.

Washington Cocktail

1½ oz. Dry Vermouth
¾ oz. Old Mr. Boston Five Star Brandy
2 Dashes Bitters
½ Teaspoon Simple Syrup
Stir well with cracked ice and strain into 3 oz. cocktail glass.

Waterbury Cocktail

½ Teaspoon Powdered Sugar
Juice of ¼ Lemon or ½ Lime
White of 1 Egg
1½ oz. Old Mr. Boston Five Star Brandy
½ Teaspoon Grenadine
Shake well with cracked ice and strain into 4 oz. cocktail glass.

Webster Cocktail

Juice ½ Lime
¼ oz. Old Mr. Boston Apricot Flavored Brandy
½ oz. Dry Vermouth
1 oz. Old Mr. Boston Dry Gin
Shake well with cracked ice and strain into 3 oz. cocktail glass.

Wedding Belle Cocktail

¼ oz. Orange Juice
¼ oz. Old Mr. Boston Wild Cherry Flavored Brandy
¾ oz. Old Mr. Boston Dry Gin
¾ oz. Dubonnet
Shake well with cracked ice and strain into 3 oz. cocktail glass.

---

* *Bourbon, Blended, Rye or Canadian.*

Weep No More Cocktail

Juice ½ Lime
¾ oz. Dubonnet
¾ oz. Old Mr. Boston Five Star Brandy
¼ Teaspoon Maraschino
Shake well with cracked ice and strain into 3 oz. cocktail glass.

Wembley Cocktail

¾ oz. Dry Vermouth
1½ oz. Old Mr. Boston Dry Gin
¼ Teaspoon Old Mr. Boston Apricot Flavored Brandy
½ Teaspoon Apple Brandy
Stir well with cracked ice and strain into 3 oz. cocktail glass.

West Indies Frosted Cocktail

See Frozen Daiquiri Cocktail *on page 39.*

Western Rose Cocktail

½ oz. Old Mr. Boston Apricot Flavored Brandy
1 oz. Old Mr. Boston Dry Gin
½ oz. Dry Vermouth
¼ Teaspoon Lemon Juice
Shake well with cracked ice and strain into 3 oz. cocktail glass.

Whip Cocktail

½ oz. Dry Vermouth
½ oz. Sweet Vermouth
1¼ oz. Old Mr. Boston Five Star Brandy
¼ Teaspoon Absinthe Substitute
1 Teaspoon Curacao
Stir well with cracked ice and strain into 3 oz. cocktail glass.

Whiskey Cobbler

Dissolve, in 10 oz. goblet,
1 Teaspoon Powdered Sugar
2 oz. Carbonated Water
Fill goblet with shaved ice; add:
2 oz. Old Mr. Boston Whiskey*
Stir well and decorate with fruits in season. Serve with straws.

Whiskey Cocktail

1 Dash Bitters
1 Teaspoon Simple Syrup
2 oz. Old Mr. Boston Whiskey*
Stir well with cracked ice and strain into 3 oz. cocktail glass. Serve with a cherry.

Whiskey Collins

Juice of ½ Lemon
1 Teaspoon Powdered Sugar
2 oz. Old Mr. Boston Whiskey*
Shake well with cracked ice and strain into 12 oz. Tom Collins glass. Add several cubes of ice, fill with carbonated water and stir. Decorate with slice of lemon, orange and a cherry. Serve with straws.

Whiskey Daisy

Juice of ½ Lemon
½ Teaspoon Powdered Sugar
1 Teaspoon Raspberry Syrup or Grenadine
2 oz. Old Mr. Boston Whiskey*
Shake well with cracked ice and strain into stein or 8 oz. metal cup. Add cube of ice and decorate with fruit.

* *Bourbon, Blended, Rye or Canadian.*

Whiskey Eggnog

1 Egg
1 Teaspoon Powdered Sugar
2 oz. Old Mr. Boston Whiskey*
Fill glass with Milk. Shake well with cracked ice and strain into 12 oz. Tom Collins glass. Grate nutmeg on top.

Whiskey Fix

Juice of ½ Lemon
1 Teaspoon Powdered Sugar
1 Teaspoon Water and stir
Fill glass with Shaved Ice
2½ oz. Old Mr. Boston Whiskey*
Use 8 oz. highball glass. Stir well. Add slice of lemon. Serve with straws.

Whiskey Flip

1 Egg
1 Teaspoon Powdered Sugar
1½ oz. Old Mr. Boston Whiskey*
2 Teaspoons Sweet Cream (if desired)
Shake well with cracked ice and strain into 5 oz. flip glass. Grate a little nutmeg on top.

Whiskey Highball

1 Cube of Ice
2 oz. Old Mr. Boston Whiskey*
Fill 8 oz. highball glass with ginger ale or carbonated water. Add twist of lemon peel, if desired, and stir.

* Bourbon, Blended, Rye or Canadian.

Old Mr. Boston Eggnog 30 Proof ▶

W

Whiskey Milk Punch

1 Teaspoon Powdered Sugar
2 oz. Old Mr. Boston Whiskey*
½ pt. Milk
Shake well with cracked ice, strain into 12 oz. Tom Collins glass and grate nutmeg on top.

Whiskey Orange

Juice of ½ Orange
1 Teaspoon Powdered Sugar
½ Teaspoon Absinthe Substitute
1½ oz. Old Mr. Boston Whiskey*
Shake well with cracked ice and strain into 8 oz. highball glass. Decorate with slice of orange and lemon.

Whiskey Rickey

1 Cube of Ice
Juice of ½ Lime
1½ oz. Old Mr. Boston Whiskey*
Fill 8 oz. highball glass with carbonated water and stir. Leave lime in glass.

Whiskey Sangaree

Dissolve ½ teaspoon powdered sugar in 1 teaspoon of water. Add:
2 oz. Old Mr. Boston Whiskey*
2 cubes of Ice.
Serve in 8 oz. highball glass. Fill balance with soda water. Stir, leaving enough room on which to float a tablespoon of Port Wine. Sprinkle lightly with nutmeg.

Whiskey Skin

Put lump of sugar into hot whiskey glass and fill two-thirds with boiling water. Add 2 oz. Old Mr. Boston Whiskey.* *Stir, then add twist of lemon peel and drop in glass.*

Whiskey Sling

Dissolve 1 teaspoon powdered sugar in teaspoon of water and juice ½ lemon
2 oz. Old Mr. Boston Whiskey*
2 Cubes of Ice
Serve in Old Fashioned cocktail glass and stir. Twist of lemon peel and drop in glass.

Whiskey Smash

Muddle 1 lump of sugar with
1 oz. Carbonated Water and
4 Sprigs of Green Mint
Add 2 oz. Old Mr. Boston Whiskey,* then a Cube of Ice
Stir and decorate with a slice of orange and a cherry. Twist of lemon peel. Use Old Fashioned cocktail glass.

Whiskey Sour

Juice of ½ Lemon
½ Teaspoon Powdered Sugar
2 oz. Old Mr. Boston Whiskey*
Shake well with cracked ice and strain into 6 oz. sour glass. Decorate with a half-slice of lemon and a cherry.

Whiskey Squirt

1½ oz. Old Mr. Boston Whiskey*
1 Tablespoon Powdered Sugar
1 Tablespoon Raspberry Syrup or Grenadine
Shake well with cracked ice and strain into 8 oz. highball glass and fill with carbonated water. Decorate with cubes of pineapple and strawberries.

* *Bourbon, Blended, Rye or Canadian.*

W

Whiskey Swizzle

Made same as Gin Swizzle *(see page 43), using* 2 oz. Old Mr. Boston Whiskey* *instead of gin.*

Whiskey Toddy

Use Old Fashioned cocktail glass.
½ Teaspoon Powdered Sugar
2 Teaspoons Water
2 oz. Old Mr. Boston Whiskey*
1 Lump of Ice
Stir well. Twist lemon peel and drop in glass.

Whiskey Toddy (Hot)

Put lump of sugar into hot whiskey glass and fill two-thirds with boiling water. Add 2 oz. Old Mr. Boston Whiskey.* *Stir and decorate with slice of lemon. Grate nutmeg on top.*

Whispers of the Frost Cocktail

¾ oz. Old Mr. Boston Whiskey*
¾ oz. Sherry Wine
¾ oz. Port Wine
1 Teaspoon Powdered Sugar
Shake well with cracked ice and strain into 3 oz. cocktail glass. Serve with slices of lemon and orange.

White Cargo Cocktail

1 Small Scoop Vanilla Ice Cream
1 oz. Old Mr. Boston Dry Gin
Shake until thoroughly mixed and add water or Sauterne if the mixture is too thick. Serve in 4 oz. cocktail glass.

White Lady Cocktail

White of 1 Egg
1 Teaspoon Powdered Sugar
1 Teaspoon Sweet Cream
1½ oz. Old Mr. Boston Dry Gin
Shake well with cracked ice and strain into 4 oz. cocktail glass.

White Lily Cocktail

¾ oz. Triple Sec
¾ oz. Old Mr. Boston Imported Rum
¾ oz. Old Mr. Boston Dry Gin
¼ Teaspoon Old Mr. Boston Anisette
Shake well with cracked ice and strain into 3 oz. cocktail glass.

White Lion Cocktail

Juice ½ Lemon
1 Teaspoon Powdered Sugar
2 Dashes Bitters
½ Teaspoon Grenadine
1½ oz. Old Mr. Boston Imported Rum
Shake well with cracked ice and strain into 3 oz. cocktail glass.

White Plush

Pour 2 oz. Old Mr. Boston Whiskey* *into Delmonico glass. Fill balance with milk and drink without stirring.*

White Rose Cocktail

¾ oz. Old Mr. Boston Dry Gin
½ oz. Orange Juice
Juice 1 Lime
½ oz. Maraschino
White of 1 Egg
Shake well with cracked ice and strain into 4 oz. cocktail glass.

* *Bourbon, Blended, Rye or Canadian.*

WHITE WAY COCKTAIL

¾ oz. Old Mr. Boston Creme de Menthe (white)
1½ oz. Old Mr. Boston Dry Gin
Shake well with cracked ice and strain into 3 oz. cocktail glass.

WIDOW'S DREAM COCKTAIL

1½ oz. Benedictine
1 Whole Egg
Shake well with cracked ice and strain into 4 oz. cocktail glass. Float 1 teaspoon of cream on top.

WIDOW'S KISS COCKTAIL

½ oz. Yellow Chartreuse
½ oz. Benedictine
1 oz. Apple Brandy
1 Dash Bitters
Shake well with cracked ice and strain into 3 oz. cocktail glass. Strawberry may be served on top.

WINDY CORNER COCKTAIL

2 oz. Old Mr. Boston Blackberry Flavored Brandy
Stir well with cracked ice and strain into 3 oz. cocktail glass. Grate a little nutmeg on top.

XANTHIA COCKTAIL

¾ oz. Old Mr. Boston Wild Cherry Flavored Brandy
¾ oz. Yellow Chartreuse
¾ oz. Old Mr. Boston Dry Gin
Stir well with cracked ice and strain into 3 oz. cocktail glass.

XERES COCKTAIL

1 Dash Orange Bitters
2 oz. Sherry Wine
Stir well with cracked ice and strain into 3 oz. cocktail glass.

X. Y. Z. COCKTAIL

½ oz. Lemon Juice
½ oz. Triple Sec
1 oz. Old Mr. Boston Imported Rum
Shake well with cracked ice and strain into 3 oz. cocktail glass.

YALE COCKTAIL

1½ oz. Old Mr. Boston Dry Gin
½ oz. Dry Vermouth
1 Dash Bitters
1 Teaspoon Creme de Yvette
Stir well with cracked ice and strain into 3 oz. cocktail glass.

OLD
Mr.BOSTON
Fine
Liquors
Old Mr.BOSTON
PEPPERMINT
SCHNAPPS
A RARE LIQUEUR
delicate in PEPPERMINT FRAGRANCE
cooling in taste and aroma
Sixty Proof
PRODUCED AND BOTTLED BY
MR BOSTON DISTILLER INC
BOSTON, MASS
4/5 QUART
OLD
Mr.BOSTON
ROCK&RYE

X Y Z

Yellow Parrot Cocktail

¾ oz. Old Mr. Boston Anisette
¾ oz. Yellow Chartreuse
¾ oz. Old Mr. Boston Apricot Flavored Brandy

Stir well with cracked ice and strain into 3 oz. cocktail glass.

Zaza Cocktail

1½ oz. Old Mr. Boston Dry Gin
¾ oz. Dubonnet
1 Twist Orange Peel

Stir well with cracked ice and strain into 3 oz. cocktail glass.

Zero Mint

For each serving desired chill 2 oz. Old Mr. Boston Creme de Menthe (green) mixed with 1 oz. water in freezing compartment of refrigerator for 2 hours or longer if desired. (Does not have to be frozen). Serve in 3 oz. cocktail glasses.

Zombie

1 oz. Unsweetened Pineapple Juice
Juice 1 Lime
Juice 1 Small Orange
1 Teaspoon Powdered Sugar
½ oz. Old Mr. Boston Apricot Flavored Brandy
2½ oz. Old Mr. Boston Imported Rum
1 oz. Jamaica Rum
1 oz. Passion Fruit Juice may be added

Add cracked ice and agitate for full minute in electric mixing machine (if none available, shake very well in cocktail shaker), and strain into 14 oz. frosted zombie glass. Decorate with square of pineapple and 1 green and 1 red cherry.

Carefully float ½ oz. 151 proof Demerara Rum and then top with sprig of fresh Mint dipped in powdered sugar. Serve with straws.

Special Sections

Eggnog

The Martini

Bar Hints and Suggestions

The Liquor Dictionary

Eggnog

SOME PEOPLE BELIEVE that this name is of English derivation and that "nog" comes from the word "noggin," a small drinking vessel with an upright handle. On the other hand, there are those who believe that the name is a result of joining the sounds of egg 'n grog. From whatever source, the drink itself is American dating back to about 1775. In the early days, eggnog was associated with traveling and social functions. Today it is principally associated with Easter, Thanksgiving, Christmas and New Years.

Traditionally, the liquors used in eggnog have been rum and brandy. However, whiskey, sherry, ale and cider may be used. Some of the early recipes called for milking the cow into the liquor but today, fortunately, this is unnecessary as simpler methods are now available. There are excellent nonalcoholic, prepared eggnogs to which one's favorite liquor may be added. These are available during the holiday season from virtually all dairy companies. Most of the following are simplified versions of recipes listed alphabetically in this book (for those who prefer to make their own preparations). For a complete list of recipes see the Index, page 143.

MIXING INSTRUCTIONS

A smaller or greater quantity of liquor than that called for in the following recipes may be used, depending on one's preference. Best results are obtained when all ingredients have been prechilled. Stir well, sprinkle nutmeg on top and serve in 4 oz. punch cups or glasses.

Ambassador's Morning Lift

1 qt. Prepared Dairy Eggnog
6 oz. Cognac
3 oz. Jamaica Rum
3 oz. Old Mr. Boston Creme de Cacao

Old Mr. Boston Five Star Brandy *or* Old Mr. Boston Bourbon Whiskey *may be substituted for Cognac.*

Baltimore Eggnog

1 qt. Prepared Dairy Eggnog
5 oz. Old Mr. Boston Five Star Brandy
5 oz. Jamaica Rum
5 oz. Madeira Wine

Brandy Eggnog

1 qt. Prepared Dairy Eggnog
12 oz. Old Mr. Boston Five Star Brandy

Breakfast Eggnog

1 qt. Prepared Dairy Eggnog
10 oz. Old Mr. Boston Apricot Flavored Brandy
2½ oz. Curacao

Christmas Yule Eggnog

1 qt. Prepared Dairy Eggnog
12 oz. Old Mr. Boston Whiskey*
1½ oz. Old Mr. Boston Imported Rum

General Harrison's Eggnog

1 qt. Prepared Dairy Eggnog
24 oz. Sweet Cider

Imperial Eggnog

1 qt. Prepared Dairy Eggnog
10 oz. Old Mr. Boston Five Star Brandy
2 oz. Old Mr. Boston Apricot Flavored Brandy

Nashville Eggnog

1 qt. Prepared Dairy Eggnog
6 oz. Old Mr. Boston Kentucky Bourbon Whiskey
3 oz. Old Mr. Boston Five Star Brandy
3 oz. Jamaica Rum

Port Wine Eggnog

1 qt. Prepared Dairy Eggnog
18 oz. Port Wine

Rum Eggnog

1 qt. Prepared Dairy Eggnog
12 oz. Old Mr. Boston Imported Rum

Sherry Eggnog

1 qt. Prepared Dairy Eggnog
18 oz. Sherry Wine

Whiskey Eggnog

1 qt. Prepared Dairy Eggnog
12 oz. Old Mr. Boston Whiskey*

* Bourbon, Blended, Rye or Canadian

The Martini

Though the martini is viewed with almost reverent awe as a drink of unique power, it is no more or less powerful than any other drink containing the same amount of alcohol.

The original Martini recipe called for one-half dry gin and one-half dry vermouth. This proportion began to change in the early 1940s to two or three parts dry gin to one part dry vermouth. Today, popular proportions for an Extra Dry Martini range from a 5-to-1 to an 8-to-1 ratio. The greater the proportion of gin to vermouth, the "drier" the Martini.

Are Your Martinis Too Strong?

Remember, America is nearly the only country in the world that drinks high-proof gin. The British, who perfected gin, and the Canadians prefer their gin at milder, smoother 80 proof.

To make Martinis that are extra dry but not extra strong, use 80 proof gin. The chart below shows how the trend to drier Martinis has increased the alcoholic content of this popular drink from a smooth 76.5 proof to a powerful 84 proof! Today's very dry Martini can be returned to its original, more moderate proof only by using 80 proof gin.

Using Standard 36 Proof Dry Vermouth	With 90 Proof Dry Gin	Or 80 Proof Dry Gin (or Vodka)
3—to—1 (Traditional)	76.5 Proof	69.0 Proof
5—to—1 (Dry)	81.0 Proof	72.6 Proof
8—to—1 (Extra Dry)	84.0 Proof	75.1 Proof

Martini Mixing

Chill 3-ounce cocktail glasses to the point of frost. Fill Martini pitcher with cracked (not crushed) ice. Ice should be dry and hard frozen. Measure out the exact ingredients for the number of drinks required, pouring in the dry gin first (gin should "smoke" as it settles over the cold ice), then the Dry Vermouth. Stir briskly until drink is very cold. Strain at once into frosty, stemmed cocktail glasses. For Martinis "on the rocks," use pre-chilled Old-Fashioned glasses and pour the liquor over cubes of ice. A twist of lemon peel (see page 125) adds a special character to a Martini which many prefer.

The following are the more popular Martinis.

Martini (Traditional 2-to-1)
1½ oz. Old Mr. Boston Dry Gin
¾ oz. Dry Vermouth
Serve with an olive

Dry Martini (5-to-1)
1⅔ oz. Old Mr. Boston Dry Gin
⅓ oz. Dry Vermouth
Serve with an olive

Extra Dry Martini (7-to-1)
1¾ oz. Old Mr. Boston Dry Gin
¼ oz. Dry Vermouth
Serve with an olive

Martini (Sweet)
1 oz. Old Mr. Boston Dry Gin
1 oz. Sweet Vermouth
Serve with an olive.

Vodka Martini—Vodkatini
Substitute Old Mr. Boston Vodka for Old Mr. Boston Dry Gin *in any of these Martini recipes.*

Martini (Medium)
1½ oz. Old Mr. Boston Dry Gin
½ oz. Dry Vermouth
½ oz. Sweet Vermouth
Serve with an olive

Boston Bullet
A Martini substituting an olive stuffed with an almond for the regular olive.

Dillatini
A Martini substituting a Dilly Bean in place of the olive.

Gibson
This is a Dry or Extra Dry Martini with a twist of lemon peel and served with one to three pearl onions. May also be made with Old Mr. Boston Vodka.

Tequini
A Martini made with Tequila instead of dry gin. Serve with a twist of lemon peel and an olive.

Bar Hints and Measurements

Here are some suggestions and fine points that will help you mix a perfect drink every time. Follow them carefully and your drinks will have the extra added touch of artistry that will mark you as a professional.

Equipment

Here is a sensible list of basic, serviceable items for even the most professional bar.

- A jigger measure—designed with an accurate scale of half and quarter ounces
- A sturdy mixing glass or shaker
- A bar strainer
- A teaspoon or set of measuring spoons
- A glass stirring rod, or a long spoon—for mixing and stirring
- A corkscrew, can and bottle opener
- A paring knife—for paring and cutting fruit
- A vacuum-type ice bucket with tongs
- A wooden muddler—for mashing mint, herbs, fruits
- A lemon-lime squeezer
- A large pitcher—with a good pouring lip
- A variety of glassware (See inside back cover)

A Buying Guide

Use the following as a reference for determining approximately how many bottles you may need for various occasions. To be extra safe, but conservative, substitute quarts for fifths.

No. of People	For Cocktails	You'll Need at Least	For Buffet or Dinner	You'll Need at Least	For an After-Dinner Party	You'll Need at Least
4	10 to 16 drinks	1 fifth	8 cocktails 8 glasses wine 4 liqueurs 8 highballs	1 fifth 2 bottles ⅘ pint 1 fifth	12 to 16 drinks	1 fifth
6	15 to 22 drinks	2 fifths	12 cocktails 12 glasses wine 8 liqueurs 18 highballs	1 fifth 2 bottles 1 fifth 2 fifths	18 to 26 drinks	2 fifths
8	18 to 24 drinks	2 fifths	16 cocktails 16 glasses wine 10 liqueurs 18 highballs	1 fifth 3 bottles 1 fifth 2 fifths	20 to 34 drinks	2 fifths
12	20 to 40 drinks	3 fifths	24 cocktails 24 glasses wine 16 liqueurs 30 highballs	2 fifths 4 bottles 1 fifth 3 fifths	25 to 45 drinks	3 fifths
20	40 to 65 drinks	4 fifths	40 cocktails 40 glasses wine 25 liqueurs 50 highballs	3 fifths 7 bottles 2 fifths 4 fifths	45 to 75 drinks	5 fifths

Measuring

Even the most professional bartender measures the ingredients of every drink, even though experience may permit some to do this by eye and by skillful freehand pouring. However, to make a perfect drink every time, measure all ingredients. Remember, too, that many drinks can be spoiled by being too strong as well as too weak.

Some standard bar measures:

1 Dash	⅙ teaspoon (1/32 ounce)
1 Teaspoon (bar spoon)	⅛ ounce
1 Pony	1 ounce
1 Jigger (barglass)	1½ ounces
1 Wineglass	4 ounces
1 Split	6 ounces
1 Cup	8 ounces

Some other helpful measures:

1 Miniature (nip)	1, 1.6 or 2 ounces
1 Half pint (¼ quart)	8 ounces (1/16 gallon)
1 Tenth (⅘ pint)	12.8 ounces (1/10 gallon)
1 Pint (½ quart)	16 ounces (⅛ gallon)
1 Fifth (⅘ quart)	25.6 ounces (⅕ gallon)
1 Quart	32 ounces (¼ gallon)
1 Imperial Quart	38.4 ounces
1 Half gallon	64 ounces
1 Gallon	128 ounces

And some *average* dry wine and champagne bottle measures:

Split (¼ bottle)	6 to 6½ ounces
"Pint" (½ bottle)	11 to 13 ounces
"Quart" (1 bottle)	24 to 26 ounces
Magnum (2 bottles)	52 ounces
Jeroboam (4 bottles)	104 ounces
Tappit-hen	128 ounces (1 gallon)
Rehoboam (6 bottles)	156 ounces (1.22 gallons)
Methuselah (8 bottles)	208 ounces (1.625 gallons)
Salmanazar (12 bottles)	312 ounces (2.44 gallons)
Balthazar (16 bottles)	416 ounces (3.3 gallons)
Nebuchadnezzar (20 bottles)	520 ounces (4.07 gallons)
Demijohn	627.2 ounces (4.9 gallons)

Glassware

All recipes in this book indicate the size and type of glass that is appropriate for each drink. For a complete list and illustration of recommended glassware, see the inside back cover.

Always use clean sparkling glassware. Keep one towel for drying and another for polishing. A stemmed glass should be used for cold drinks served without ice, like Martinis. When held, the heat of the hand will not warm the drink as it is being consumed.

How to Chill a Glass

Cocktail glasses should be well chilled to keep the drinks refreshingly cold. If refrigerator space is not available for prechilling, fill each glass with cracked, shaved or crushed ice before mixing. When the drink is ready, empty the glass, shake out the melted ice and then pour the drink.

How to Frost a Glass

There are two types of "frosted" glass. For "frosted" drinks, glasses should be stored in a refrigerator or buried in shaved ice long enough to give each glass a white, frosted, ice-cold look and feel.

For a "sugar-frosted" glass, moisten the rim of a prechilled glass with a slice of lime or lemon and then dip the rim into powdered sugar.

Ice

Use plenty of ice. Whether cubed, cracked, crushed or shaved, all ice should be fresh, crystal-clear and free of any taste. Always put ice in the mixing glass, shaker or drinking glass before pouring any ingredients. The liquids are chilled as they are poured over the ice and there is no splashing.

Most highballs, Old Fashioneds and on-the-rocks drinks call for cubed ice. Use cracked or cubed ice for stirring and shaking; crushed or shaved ice for special tall drinks, frappés and other drinks to be sipped through straws.

Sugar

Always place sugar in the mixing glass before adding the liquor. Unless otherwise stated in the recipe, powdered sugar should be used with alcohol. Powdered sugar dissolves and blends quickest with alcohol at low temperatures.

Simple Syrup

Simple syrup may be substituted for powdered sugar in many drinks. Some bartenders claim it gives certain drinks a smoother, richer taste. Many prefer it because it blends instantly. You may make a simple syrup ahead of time and store it in bottles in a cool place. Dissolve one pound of granulated sugar in one half pint of warm water, gradually stirring in enough water to make one pint of syrup.

When to Stir

Drinks containing clear liquors and ingredients require stirring with ice for proper mixing. Stir drinks containing a carbonated mixer (tonic water, ginger ale, cola, etc.) *gently* to preserve the sparkle and effervescence. Remember, too little stirring fails to mix or chill the ingredients; too much stirring melts the ice and dilutes the drink.

When to Shake

Drinks containing fruit juices, sugar, eggs, cream or other ingredients difficult to mix, should be shaken briskly. For thorough blending of some punches, sours, other fruit and egg drinks, and where frothiness is desired, use an electric mixer or blender.

Using the Strainer

Strain all cocktails before serving with a wire—not silver—strainer. Use one with clips that permits the wire to rest within the rim of the mixing glass or shaker.

Pouring

When mixing the same cocktail for four or more people, make the drinks in one batch. To make each drink of equal strength and taste set up the required number of glasses in a row. Pour, filling each glass only halfway. Then go back to the first glass and finish off.

How to Float Cordials

To make cordials or brandy float one on top of the other in the same glass, as in the Pousse Café, pour each ingredient slowly over a teaspoon held bottom side up over the glass. The rounded surface of the teaspoon will spread each cordial or brandy slowly and evenly over the one below without mixing. This may also be accomplished by first inserting a glass stirring rod into the glass and then slowly pouring each ingredient down the rod.

Be sure to pour all ingredients in the order given in the recipe.

How to Flame Liquor

The secret to setting liquor (brandy, rum, gin, whiskey) aflame in drink and cooking recipes is to make certain that glass, cooking vessel and liquor are all prewarmed. Start with a teaspoon or tablespoon of liquor, preheat over flame, then set afire. Pour flaming liquid carefully into remaining liquor to be set aflame.

Using Eggs

To separate the white of an egg from the yellow, break the egg by hitting the center on the edge of a glass. Separate the two halves, passing the yolk from one half-shell to the other until the white slips through to the glass below.

The egg always goes into the mixing glass or shaker before the liquor, to make certain that the egg is fresh. When shaking, use cubed or cracked ice to break up and blend the egg with the other ingredients.

Using Fruit and Fruit Juices

Whenever possible use only *fresh* fruit. Wash the outside peel before using. Fruit slices should be cut about one-quarter-inch thick and slit toward the center to fix slice on rim of glass. Keep garnishes fresh and cold.

When mixing drinks containing fruit juices, *always* pour the liquor last. Squeeze and strain fruit juices just before using to insure freshness and good taste. Avoid artificial, concentrated substitutes.

Twist of Lemon Peel

When recipes call for a twist of lemon peel, rub a narrow strip of peel around the rim of the glass to deposit the oil on it. Then twist the peel so that the oil (usually one small drop) will drop into the drink. Then drop in the peel. The lemon oil gives added character to the cocktail which many prefer.

Using Bitters

Ordinarily, only a dash or two is necessary. This small but important ingredient can add zest to a great number of mixed drinks. Made from numerous and subtle combinations of roots, barks, berries and herbs, they are all characterized by their aromatic, bitter taste.

Here are a few of the best-known brands:

Angostura Bitters—made in Trinidad from an ancient, secret recipe.

Abbott's Aged Bitters—made in Baltimore by the same family since 1865.

Peychaud's Bitters—made in New Orleans.

Orange Bitters—made from the dried peel of bitter Seville oranges and sold by several English firms.

Vermouth

Vermouth is a white appetizer wine flavored with as many as thirty to forty different herbs, roots, berries, flowers and seeds. There are nearly as many vermouth formulas as there are brand labels.

The dry variety (French) is light gold in color and has a delightful nutty flavor. Sweet (Italian) vermouth is richer in flavor and more syrupy. Both are delicate and will lose their freshness if left too long in an opened bottle. Use with care and discretion in mixed drinks (follow the recipe) since most people now prefer "drier" cocktails.

The Liquor Dictionary

MUCH of the enjoyment of social drinking comes from a knowledge of the different types of alcoholic beverages available. This section was prepared to help you understand some of the, ofttimes subtle, differences between one type of liquor and another.

First, here are a few common terms frequently misunderstood:

ALCOHOL (C_2H_5OH) the common ingredient of all liquor. There are many types of alcohol, but for beverages only ethyl alcohol is used. Of the several types of ethyl alcohol, those spirits distilled from grain, grape, fruit and cane are the most common.

PROOF–a measurement of alcoholic strength or content. One de gree of proof equals one-half of 1 per cent of alcohol. An 80 proof product contains 40 per cent alcohol; a 90 proof product, 45 per cent alcohol, etc.

For centuries Scotch, British Gin and Canadian Whisky sold in England, Scotland, Canada and most of the rest of the world has been sold at mild 80 proof. America has only begun to appreciate the tasteful qualities of the more moderate lower proofs.

In recent years, a trend has developed in this country toward 80 proof blended and straight whiskeys, dry gin, Scotch and Canadian whiskies. Practically all of the *Rum* sold in America is now 80 proof. *Vodka* at 80 proof outsells the higher proofs 9-to-1. For years the most expensive, famous-name Cognacs have been imported at 80 proof, and now nearly all American-made *Brandy* is 80 proof.

AGE—often believed to be the *only* indication of quality; a whiskey, rum, or brandy can be aged too long as well as not long enough. Other factors affecting quality include variables in the distilling process itself, the types of grain used, the warehousing techniques employed, the rate of aging and the degree of skill used in determining product maturity. Aging may make good whiskey better, but no amount of aging can make good whiskey out of bad.

GRAIN NEUTRAL SPIRITS—a practically tasteless, colorless alcohol distilled from grain (like whiskey) but at 190 proof or above, whereas whiskey must be distilled at less than 190 proof. Used in blended whiskeys, in making gin and vodka, and in many other liquors.

WINE—produced principally from the fermented juice of grapes. If any other fruit is used, the name of the fruit must appear on the label. The alcoholic content of wine ranges from less than 14 per cent to 21 per cent.

BEER—the name for five types of fermented malt beverages: *Lager Beer* (about 3.6 per cent alcohol), the most popular type of light, dry beer; *Ale,* having a more pronounced flavor and aroma of hops, is heavier and more bitter than lager beer; *Bock Beer, Porter* and *Stout* (about 6 per cent alcohol), which are progressively heavier, darker, richer and sweeter than either lager beer or ale.

Brandy

BRANDY IS DISTILLED from a fermented mash of grapes or other fruit. These brandies, aged in oak casks, are usually bottled at either 80 or 84 proof. Long enjoyed as an after-dinner drink, brandy is also widely used in cooking.

COGNAC—this fine brandy, known for its smoothness and heady dry aroma, is produced only in the Cognac region of France. (All Cognac is brandy, but not all brandy is Cognac, nor is all French brandy Cognac.)

ARMAGNAC—is much like Cognac but has a drier taste. It is produced only in the Armagnac region of France.

AMERICAN BRANDY—all of which is distilled in California, has its own excellent characteristics of taste. Unlike European brandies (whose farmer-distillers sell their brandies to blender-shippers who control the brand names), California brandies are usually produced by individual firms that grow the grapes, distill, age, blend, bottle and market the brandies under their own brand names.

APPLE BRANDY, APPLE JACK or CALVADOS—is distilled from a cider made from apples. Calvados is produced only in Normandy, France. Apple Jack may be bottled-in-bond under the same regulations that apply to whiskey.

FRUIT-FLAVORED BRANDIES—are brandy-based liqueurs produced from Blackberries, Peaches, Apricots, Cherries and Ginger. They are usually bottled at 70 or 80 proof.

Cordials

The words Cordial and Liqueur are synonymous, describing liquors made by mixing or redistilling neutral spirits with fruits, flowers, herbs, seeds, roots, plants or juices to which sweetening has been added. Practically all cordials are sweet and colorful, with highly concentrated, dessertlike flavor.

Cordials are made in all countries. Several, made from closely guarded secret recipes and processes, are known throughout the world by their trade or proprietary brand names.

Here are brief descriptions of the cordials and flavorings mentioned most frequently in the recipes in this book:

ABSINTHE—anise seed (licorice) flavor; contains wormwood; illegal in the United States

ABSINTHE SUBSTITUTES—Abisante, Abson, Anisette, Herbsaint, Mistra, Ojen, Oxygene, Pernod

AMER PICON—bitter, orange-flavored French cordial made from quinine and spices

ANISETTE—anise seed, licorice flavor

BENEDICTINE—secret herb formula first produced by Benedictine monks

BITTERS—(see page 125)

CHARTREUSE—yellow and green herb liqueurs developed by Carthusian monks

CREME(S)—so-called because high sugar content results in cream-like consistency

    CREME DE CACAO—from cacao and vanilla beans

    CREME DE CASSIS—from black currants

    CREME DE MENTHE—from mint

    CREME DE YVETTE—from violets

CURACAO—orange-flavored, made of dried orange peel, from Dutch West Indies

DUBONNET—French aperitif wine made from aromatics, has slight quinine taste

GRENADINE—made from pomegranates, used for flavoring

KUMMEL—caraway and anise seeds and other herb flavors

MARASCHINO—liqueur made from cherries grown in Dalmatia, Yugoslavia

PASSION FRUIT (PASSIONOLA)—a nonalcoholic mix made from the Passion Flower

PEPPERMINT SCHNAPPS—a light-bodied creme de menthe

PERNOD—a French anise-flavored liqueur and absinthe substitute

ROCK AND RYE—fruit juice, rock candy and rye whiskey, bottled with fruit slices

SLOE GIN—a liqueur made from sloe berries (blackthorn bush)

SWEDISH PUNCH—Scandinavian liqueur made from Batavia Arak rum, tea, lemon and other spices. Also known as Arrack Punsch and Caloric Punsch (the latter because it gives off heat)

TEQUILA—a colorless Mexican liquor made from the mescal plant. Not to be confused with Pulque, made from the same plant, but with a heavy sour milk flavor.

TRIPLE SEC—colorless Curacao, but less sweet.

Gin

GIN, which is distilled from grain, receives its flavor and aroma from juniper berries and other botanicals. (Every gin producer has his own special recipe.)

Most gin is colorless, though some brands may be golden or straw-yellow because of aging in barrels. Even though a distiller ages his gin, he cannot, by law, make age claims for his product. Gin sold around the world at 80 proof is bottled in this country at proofs varying from 80 to 94.

DRY GIN—merely signifies that the gin lacks sweetness.

VACUUM-DISTILLED DRY GIN—is distilled in a glass-lined vacuum still at a low 90° Fahrenheit temperature (instead of at the usual 212°), capturing only the light, volatile flavors and aromas without the bitterness found in some gins.

LONDON DRY GIN—originated in England and is now considered a generic term and may appear on American-made gins as well. Dry gins from England are inclined to be a little heavier-bodied.

GOLDEN GIN—is a dry gin which, due to aging in wood, has acquired a golden color.

HOLLAND, GENEVA OR SCHIEDAM GINS—are imported from Holland, where gin originated, are highly flavored and rich in aromatic oils; they do not mix well with other ingredients in cocktails.

OLD TOM GIN—is an English gin that has been sweetened with sugar syrup.

FLAVORED GIN—is a sweet gin usually flavored with orange, lemon or mint.

SLOE GIN—is not a gin at all but a liqueur. (See page 130.)

Rum

Rum is distilled from the fermented juice of sugar cane, cane syrup and molasses at less than 190 proof (160 proof for New England rum) and bottled at not less than 80 proof. It is aged in uncharred barrels where it picks up very little coloring; dark rums often have caramel added to them for color.

Most rums are blends of several aged rums, ranging from heavy, pungent types to light, brandylike varieties, selected for special aroma, flavor and color. There are two main types of rum:

LIGHT-BODIED RUMS—are dry with only a very slight molasses flavor. Available in two varieties, White and Gold Label (or Light and Dark), the Gold or Dark is usually a bit sweeter with a more pronounced taste. Among these rums are included rums from Puerto Rico, Cuba and the Virgin Islands. Light-bodied rums are also produced in the Dominican Republic, Haiti, Venezuela, Mexico, Hawaii and the Philippines.

HEAVY-BODIED RUMS—are darker, sweeter and have a pungent bouquet, body and flavor. These are distilled by a different and slower fermentation process, which allows more time for a fuller, richer molasseslike body to develop and include rums from Jamaica, Demerara (British Guiana), Martinique, Trinidad, Barbados and New England.

Vodka

VODKA, most versatile of all alcoholic beverages, is a highly refined and filtered liquor distilled from any material at or above 190 proof, bottled at not less than 80 or more than 110 proof. It was originally made in Russia, from potatoes; but in the United States, vodka is usually distilled from grain, primarily corn and wheat. The subtle differences between various vodkas results from the types of grain used and the distilling and filtering processes employed. Most American vodkas are filtered through activated charcoal.

Vodka is not aged; it is colorless and virtually tasteless and odorless. In Russia and the Baltic countries, vodka is always taken straight and ice-cold from small glasses, at one swallow, along with food. In America, vodka is usually mixed with fruit juices, carbonated beverages and other ingredients where vodka's softness and palatability does not interfere with the taste of the main ingredient.

FLAVORED VODKA—an American-originated product. Excellent straight or in mixed drinks, it has been sweetened and flavored, usually with orange, lemon, lime, mint or grape. It is usually bottled at 70 proof.

ZUBROVKA—vodka in which a bit of special "buffalo" grass is steeped. This European grass gives the vodka a light yellowish color and a slight aromatic bouquet. It can be made at home by buying "buffalo" grass from an herb company and steeping it in vodka. Zubrovka is used like Vodka.

Whiskey

WHISKEYS are distilled from a fermented mash of grain (usually corn, rye, barley or wheat), and then aged in oak barrels. In this country, whiskey must be distilled at less than 190 proof (although whiskey with a specific designation such as Bourbon, Rye, etc., cannot be distilled above 160 proof) and must be bottled at no less than 80 proof.

Whiskey, when placed in barrels to age, is a water-colored liquid. It is during the aging period that whiskey obtains its characteristic amber color, flavor and aroma.

The major whiskey-producing countries are the United States, Canada, Scotland and Ireland. Special grain characteristics, recipes and distillation processes make the whiskey of each country distinct from that of the others.

AMERICAN WHISKEY—Although American whiskeys fall into two major categories, straight whiskey and blended whiskey, the United States Government acknowledges thirty-three distinct types of whiskey. Only the major types (98 per cent of the nation's consumption) are covered here.

Straight Whiskey is distilled from corn, rye, barley or wheat (not blended with neutral grain spirits or any other whiskey) and aged in charred oak barrels for a minimum of two years. There are four major types of straight whiskey:

1. *Bourbon Whiskey* is distilled from a mash of grain containing not less than 51 per cent corn and is normally aged four years in new charred oak barrels. Bourbon is amber in color and full-bodied in flavor. When distilled in Kentucky it is usually referred to as *Kentucky Straight Bourbon Whiskey*. Bourbon is named for Bourbon County in Kentucky where this type of whiskey originated. Bourbon is also produced in Illinois, Indiana, Ohio, Pennsylvania, Tennessee and Missouri.

2. *Rye Whiskey* is distilled from a mash of grain containing not less than 51 per cent rye and is much like bourbon in color, but it is different in taste and heavier in flavor.

3. *Corn Whiskey* is distilled from a mash of grain containing not less than 80 per cent corn. Corn whiskey is commonly aged in re-used charred oak barrels.

4. *Bottled-in-Bond Whiskey* is straight whiskey, usually bourbon or rye, which is produced under United States Government supervision. Though the government does not guarantee the quality of bonded whiskey, it does require that the whiskey be at least four years old, that it be bottled at 100 proof, that it be produced in one distilling by the same distiller, and that it be stored and bottled at a bonded warehouse under government supervision.

Blended Whiskey—A blend of one or more straight whiskeys and neutral grain spirits containing at least 20 per cent or more straight whiskey bottled at not less than 80 proof.

1. *Kentucky Whiskey—A Blend* is a blended whiskey in which all the straight whiskeys are distilled in Kentucky.

2. *A Blend of Straight Whiskeys* occurs when two or more straight whiskeys are blended together, to the exclusion of neutral grain spirits.

CANADIAN WHISKY—Canadian whiskies are blended whiskies, usually distilled from rye, corn and barley. Produced only in Canada, under government supervision, most of the Canadian whisky sold in this country is at least four years old. Canadian whisky, usually lighter bodied than American whiskey, is sold in Canada, and in most of the world, except the United States, at 80 proof.

SCOTCH WHISKY—Produced only in Scotland, Scotch whiskies are blended whiskies deriving their individual personalities from native barley grain and traditional pot stills. All Scotch blends contain malt whisky and grain whisky (similar to American grain neutral spirits). Scotch's distinctive smoky flavor comes from drying malted barley over peat fires. All the Scotch imported into this country is at least four years old and is usually 80 or 86 proof. Scotch sold in the rest of the world is almost always 80 proof.

IRISH WHISKEY—Produced only in Ireland, Irish whiskey, like Scotch, is a blended whiskey containing both barley malt whiskeys and grain whiskeys. Unlike Scotch, however, the malt is dried in coal-fired kilns and the aroma of the fires does not reach the malt. Irish whiskey is heavier and more full-bodied than Scotch and is usually 86 proof.

Index

If you know the name of the mixed drink you desire, you need not use this index, as all drinks are listed alphabetically throughout the book.

This index is arranged so that you may choose specific types of drinks such as cocktails, fizzes, highballs, etc., or cocktails made with Vodka, Gin, Whiskey, Sloe Gin and other ingredients.

ABSINTHE SUBSTITUTE DRINKS

Absinthe Cocktail	1
Absinthe Drip	1
Absinthe Special	1
Blarney Stone	9
Bombay Cocktail	12
Brazil Cocktail	17
Button Hook	20
Café de Paris Cocktail	21
Deep Sea Cocktail	30
Dempsey Cocktail	30
Dixie Cocktail	31
Dubarry Cocktail	32
Duchess Cocktail	32
Eyeopener Cocktail	34
Hasty Cocktail	45
Irish Whiskey Cocktail	50
Jeyplak Cocktail	52
Knock-out Cocktail	55
Ladies' Cocktail	56
Lawhill Cocktail	56
Linstead Cocktail	59
Merry Widow No. 1	63
Modern Cocktail	65
Morning Cocktail	66
Morning Glory Fizz	66
Peggy Cocktail	73
Phoebe Snow Cocktail	73
Piccadilly Cocktail	73
Presto Cocktail	78
Rattlesnake Cocktail	80
Robert E. Lee Cooler	81
Saucy Sue Cocktail	87
Sazerac Cocktail	87
Special Rough Cocktail	93
Suissesse Cocktail	95
Swiss Family Cocktail	96
Temptation Cocktail	96
Third Degree Cocktail	97
Third Rail Cocktail	97
T. N. T. Cocktail	100
Turf Cocktail	101
Tuxedo Cocktail	101
Ulanda Cocktail	101
Whip Cocktail	106
Whiskey Orange	108

ADES

These are perfect warm weather drinks, served tall and frosty with plenty of ice and garnished with slices of fruit. They are made primarily with sweetened lemon or lime juice and a variety of liquors and may be filled with plain or soda water.

California Lemonade	21
Lemon Squash	57
Lemonade (Carbonated)	57
Lemonade (Claret)	57
Lemonade (Egg)	57
Lemonade (Fruit)	57
Lemonade (Golden)	57
Lemonade (Modern)	59
Lemonade (Plain)	59
Limeade	59
Orange Smile	71
Orangeade	71

ANISETTE DRINKS

Absinthe Cocktail	1
Baltimore Bracer	5
Dream Cocktail	32
Johnnie Cocktail	52
Ladies' Cocktail	56
Shanghai Cocktail	89
Snowball Cocktail	92
Suissesse Cocktail	95
White Lily Cocktail	109
Yellow Parrot Cocktail	112

APPLE BRANDY DRINKS

Apple Blow Fizz	3
Apple Brandy Cocktail	4
Apple Brandy Highball	4
Apple Brandy Rickey	4
Apple Brandy Sour	4
Barton Special Cocktail	7
Bolero Cocktail	10
Deauville Cocktail	30
Dempsey Cocktail	30
Harvard Cooler	45
Honeymoon Cocktail	47
Jack-in-the-Box Cocktail	50
Jack Rose Cocktail	50
Jersey Lightning	51

Liberty Cocktail	59
Prince's Smile Cocktail	78
Royal Smile Cocktail	82
Saucy Sue Cocktail	87
Soother Cocktail	92
Special Rough Cocktail	93
Star Cocktail	95
Star Daisy	95
Third Rail Cocktail	97
Tulip Cocktail	101
Wembley Cocktail	106
Widow's Kiss Cocktail	110

APRICOT BRANDY DRINKS

After Dinner Cocktail	1
After Supper Cocktail	2
Apple Pie Cocktail	4
Apricot Brandy Rickey	4
Apricot Cocktail	4
Apricot Cooler	4
Apricot Fizz	4
Babbie's Special	5
Banana Punch	7
Bermuda Bouquet	8
Bermuda Rose	8
Boston Cocktail	12
Breakfast Eggnog	17, 115
Button Hook Cocktail	20
Claridge Cocktail	25
Cuban Cocktail No. 2	29
Darb Cocktail	30
English Rose Cocktail	34
Ethel Duffy Cocktail	34
Fairy Bell Cocktail	36
Favourite Cocktail	37
Fifth Avenue	37
Flamingo Cocktail	38
Frankenjack Cocktail	38
Golden Slipper Cocktail	43
Hop Toad Cocktail	47
Imperial Eggnog	115
K. C. B. Cocktail	53
Leave It To Me No. 1	57
Midnight Cocktail	64
Paradise Cocktail	72
Prince's Smile Cocktail	78
Princess Pousse Café	78
Resolute Cocktail	81

Rose Cocktail (English)	82
Saucy Sue Cocktail	87
Spencer Cocktail	93
Tempter Cocktail	96
Thanksgiving Special	97
Tulip Cocktail	101
Valencia Cocktail	103
Webster Cocktail	105
Wembley Cocktail	106
Western Rose Cocktail	106
Yellow Parrot Cocktail	112
Zombie	112

BENEDICTINE DRINKS

B & B	5
Bobby Burns Cocktail	10
Brighton Punch	18
Cabaret Cocktail	20
Frisco Sour	39
Froupe Cocktail	39
Honeymoon Cocktail	47
Honolulu No. 2	47
Hoot Mon Cocktail	47
Kentucky Colonel	53
Merry Widow No. 1	63
Pousse L'Amour	78
Preakness Cocktail	78
Queen Elizabeth	79
Rolls Royce Cocktail	81
Vodka Gypsy Cocktail	104
Widow's Dream	110
Widow's Kiss Cocktail	110

BLACKBERRY BRANDY DRINKS

Poop Deck Cocktail	76
Windy Corner Cocktail	110

BLENDED WHISKEY DRINKS

(See Whiskey Drinks, on page 147 of Index)

BOURBON WHISKEY DRINKS

(See Whiskey Drinks, on page 147 of Index)

BRANDY DRINKS

Alabama Cocktail	2
Alexander No. 2	2
Ambassador's Morning Lift	115
American Beauty	3
Angel's Kiss	3
Angel's Wing	3
B & B	5
Baltimore Bracer	5
Baltimore Eggnog	5, 115
Bermuda Highball	8
Between the Sheets	8
Bombay Cocktail	12
Bombay Punch	12
Boston Side Car	12
Brandy and Soda	13
Brandy Blazer	13
Brandy Cobbler	13
Brandy Cocktail	13
Brandy Collins	13
Brandy Crusta Cocktail	14
Brandy Daisy	14
Brandy Eggnog	14, 115
Brandy Fix	14
Brandy Fizz	14
Brandy Flip	14
Brandy Gump Cocktail	14
Brandy Highball	16
Brandy Julep	16
Brandy Milk Punch	16
Brandy Punch	16
Brandy Sangaree	16
Brandy Sling	16
Brandy Smash	17
Brandy Sour	17
Brandy Squirt	17
Brandy Swizzle	17
Brandy Toddy	17
Brandy Toddy (Hot)	17
Brandy Vermouth	17
Brighton Punch	18
Bull's Eye	20
Bull's Milk	20
Button Hook Cocktail	20
Café Royal	21
Cardinal Punch	21
Carrol Cocktail	21
Champagne Cup	22

Champagne Punch....	22
Champs Élysées......	22
Charles Cocktail......	22
Cherry Blossom......	23
Chicago Cocktail.....	23
Chocolate Daisy......	24
Chocolate Flip.......	24
Cider Cup...........	24
Claret Cup..........	25
Claret Punch.........	25
Classic Cocktail......	25
Coffee Cocktail.......	26
Coffee Flip..........	26
Cold Deck Cocktail...	26
Cuban Cocktail No. 2..	29
Deauville Cocktail....	30
Diana Cocktail.......	31
Dream Cocktail......	32
East India No. 1......	33
Egg Sour	33
English Highball.....	34
Fancy Brandy Cocktail.	36
Fantasio Cocktail.....	36
Fish House Punch.....	37
Froupe Cocktail	39
Glögg	43
Harvard Cocktail.....	45
Hot Brandy Flip......	48
Imperial Eggnog......	115
Jamaica Granito......	51
Loving Cup..........	60
Luxury Cocktail......	60
Metropolitan.........	63
Mikado Cocktail......	64
Morning Cocktail.....	66
Nashville Eggnog.....	115
Olympic Cocktail.....	69
Panama Cocktail......	72
Phoebe Snow Cocktail.	73
Poop Deck Cocktail...	76
Port Wine Cocktail....	77
Port Wine Sangaree...	77
Pousse Café..........	77
Pousse L'Amour......	78
Presto Cocktail.......	78
Quaker's Cocktail.....	79
Rhine Wine Cup.....	81
Saratoga Cocktail ...	86
Sauterne Cup........	87
Sherry Twist Cocktail.	90
Shriner Cocktail......	90
Sidecar Cocktail......	90
Sir Walter Cocktail...	91
Sloppy Joe's No. 2....	92
Soother Cocktail......	92
Special Rough Cocktail	93
Stinger Cocktail......	95
Third Rail Cocktail...	97
Three Miller Cocktail.	99
Thunder Cocktail.....	99
Thunder and Lightning	99
Thunderclap Cocktail.	99
Tom and Jerry.......	100
Vanderbilt Cocktail...	103
Washington Cocktail..	105
Waterbury Cocktail...	105
Weep No More.......	106
Whip Cocktail.......	106

CANADIAN WHISKY DRINKS

(See Whiskey Drinks, on page 147 of Index)

CHAMPAGNE DRINKS

Black Velvet.........	9
Bombay Punch.......	12
Bucks Fizz..........	18
Cardinal Punch......	21
Champagne Cocktail..	22
Champagne Cup......	22
Champagne Punch....	22
Champagne Velvet....	22
Duké Cocktail........	32
French "75".........	38
London Special......	59
Luxury Cocktail......	60
Monte Carlo Imperial Highball..........	65

CHARTREUSE DRINKS
(Green)

Bijou Cocktail.......	8
Everybody's Irish.....	34
Jewel Cocktail.......	52
Pousse Café	77
St. Patrick's Day......	86
Sand-Martin Cocktail..	86
Spring Feeling Cocktail	93
Tailspin Cocktail.....	96
Tipperary Cocktail....	100

CHARTREUSE DRINKS
(Yellow)

Alaska Cocktail.......	2
Champs Élysées.......	22
Chocolate Cocktail....	24
Golden Slipper Cocktail	43
Pousse Café..........	77
Xanthia Cocktail.....	110
Widow's Kiss Cocktail.	110
Yellow Parrot Cocktail.	112

COBBLERS

These tall drinks are generally served in a large goblet. They are made with lots of shaved ice, fruit and liquor, decorated with berries, fresh fruit and, if desired, a sprig of mint. Serve with straws.

Brandy Cobbler......	13
Claret Cobbler.......	25
Gin Cobbler.........	40
Port Wine Cobbler....	77
Rum Cobbler........	84
Sherry Cobbler.......	89
Whiskey Cobbler.....	106

COLLINS

These are tall, cool drinks belonging to the Punch family, with Tom and John the best known members. Any basic liquor can be used, with the juice of lemon or lime, over ice cubes in a frosted, 12 oz. highball glass, with sugar added to taste and filled with soda water. Garnish with a slice of lemon and a cherry.

Brandy Collins.......	13
John Collins.........	52
Mint Collins.........	64
Orange Gin Collins...	69
Rum Collins.........	84
Sloe Gin Collins......	91
Tequila Collins......	97
Tom Collins.........	100
Vodka Collins........	103
Whiskey Collins......	106

Coolers

A cooler is a tall, warm-weather drink not unlike an individual Punch except that less lemon or lime juice is used in a Cooler (usually just fruit rinds). They are made with different types of liquor, flavoring, cracked ice and a carbonated beverage.

Apricot Cooler	4
Boston Cooler	12
Country Club Cooler	28
Floradora Cooler	38
Gin Cooler	40
Harvard Cooler	45
Highland Cooler	46
Klondike Cooler	55
Lone Tree Cooler	60
Pike's Peak Cooler	73
Pineapple Cooler	73
Remsen Cooler	80
Robert E. Lee Cooler	81
Rum Cooler	84
Saratoga Cooler	86
Scotch Cooler	87
Vodka Cooler	104

Cream de Cacao Drinks (Regular)

Alexander No. 1	2
Alexander No. 2	2
Ambassador's Morning Lift	115
Angel's Kiss	3
Angel's Tip	3
Angel's Wing	3
Barbary Coast Cocktail	7
Eyeopener Cocktail	34
Fifth Avenue	37
Fox River Cocktail	38
Jockey Club Cocktail	52
Kretchma Cocktail	55
Mikado Cocktail	64
Ninitchka Cocktail	68
Panama Cocktail	72
Poppy Cocktail	76
Russian Bear Cocktail	85
Russian Cocktail	85
Tropical Cocktail	100

Creme de Cacao Drinks (White)

Flying Grasshopper	38
Grasshopper Cocktail	44
Pink Squirrel Cocktail	74
Vodka Grasshopper	104

Creme de Menthe Drinks (Green)

Alexander's Sister	2
Creme de Menthe Frappe	29
Emerald Isle	34
Everybody's Irish	34
Flying Grasshopper	38
Grasshopper Cocktail	44
Green Dragon Cocktail	44
Green Fizz	44
Green Swizzle	44
Mint Highball	64
Mint on Rocks	65
Port and Starboard	77
St. Patrick's Day	86
Shamrock Cocktail	89
Vodka Grasshopper	104
Zero Mint	112

Creme de Menthe Drinks (White)

American Beauty	3
Button Hook Cocktail	20
Cold Deck Cocktail	26
Creme de Gin	29
Diana Cocktail	31
Dixie Whiskey Cocktail	31
Ethel Duffy Cocktail	34
Fallen Angel Cocktail	36
Fantasio Cocktail	36
Knock-Out Cocktail	55
Monte Carlo Imperial	65
Pink Whiskers Cocktail	74
Pousse Café	77
Scotch Cooler	87
Stinger Cocktail	95
Vodka Stinger	104
White Way Cocktail	110

Creme de Yvette Drinks

Angel's Delight	3
Angel's Kiss	3
Blue Devil Cocktail	10
Blue Moon Cocktail	10
Crystal Slipper Cocktail	29
Orchid Cocktail	71
Ping Pong Cocktail	74
Pousse Café	77
Stars and Stripes	95
Union Jack Cocktail	101
Violet Fizz	103
Yale Cocktail	110

Cups

These delectable wine cocktails are made with Brandy and Curacao mixed with sweet wine, dry Champagne or cider. Make in glass pitchers with ice cubes and serve in stemmed claret glasses.

Champagne Cup	22
Cider Cup	24
Claret Cup	25
Loving Cup	60
Rhine Wine Cup	81
Sauterne Cup	87

Curacao Drinks

After Dinner Cocktail	1
After Supper Cocktail	2
Alabama Cocktail	2
Baron Cocktail	7
Bermuda Bouquet	8
Blarney Stone	9
Bombay Cocktail	12
Bombay Punch	12
Brandy Crusta	14
Brandy Punch	16
Breakfast Eggnog	17, 115
Broken Spur Cocktail	18
Champagne Cup	22
Champagne Punch	22

Cherry Blossom	23
Chicago Cocktail	23
Chinese Cocktail	23
Cider Cup	24
Claret Cup	25
Claret Punch	25
Classic Cocktail	25
Cuban Special Cocktail	29
Damn-the-Weather	30
Derby Fizz	31
Dixie Whiskey	31
Dream Cocktail	32
East India No. 1	33
Egg Sour	33
Ethel Duffy Cocktail	34
Eyeopener Cocktail	34
Fair and Warmer	36
Fancy Brandy Cocktail	36
Fancy Gin Cocktail	36
Fancy Whiskey Cocktail	36
Hawaiian Cocktail	46
Honeymoon Cocktail	47
Ice Cream Flip	49
Irish Whiskey Cocktail	50
Jamaica Granito	51
Johnnie Cocktail	52
Journalist Cocktail	52
Knickerbocker Special	55
Maiden's Blush	61
Mai-Tai	61
Martinez Cocktail	62
McClelland Cocktail	63
Midnight Cocktail	64
Mikado Cocktail	64
Millionaire Cocktail	64
Morning Cocktail	66
Napolean Cocktail	67
Olympic Cocktail	69
Oriental Cocktail	71
Parisian Blonde Cocktail	72
Planter's Punch No. 2	76
Rhine Wine Cup	81
Sauterne Cup	87
Sir Walter Cocktail	91
Sloppy Joe's No. 1	92
Sloppy Joe's No. 2	92
Soother Cocktail	92
Southern Gin Cocktail	93
Spanish Town Cocktail	93
Tango Cocktail	96
Temptation Cocktail	96
Wallick Cocktail	105

Whip Cocktail	106

DAISIES

These overgrown cocktails are made of liquor, grenadine (or other cordials), and lemon or lime juice. Usually shaken with cracked ice, they are served in a stein, metal cup or Old Fashioned glass over an ice cube and decorated with fruit.

	14
Brandy Daisy	24
Chocolate Daisy	40
Gin Daisy	84
Rum Daisy	95
Star Daisy	104
Vodka Daisy	106
Whiskey Daisy	

DRY GIN DRINKS

Abbey Cocktail	1
Alabama Fizz	2
Alaska Cocktail	2
Albemarle Fizz	2
Alexander No. 1	2
Alexander's Sister	2
Allen Cocktail	2
Allies Cocktail	2
Apricot Cocktail	4
Babbie's Special	5
Bachelor's Bait Cocktail	5
Barbary Coast Cocktail	7
Baron Cocktail	7
Beauty Spot Cocktail	7
Belmont Cocktail	7
Bennett Cocktail	7
Bermuda Bouquet	8
Bermuda Highball	8
Bermuda Rose Cocktail	8
Biffy Cocktail	8
Bijou Cocktail	8
Billy Taylor	8
Bird of Paradise Fizz	8
Blood Bronx Cocktail	9
Bloodhound Cocktail	9
Blue Devil Cocktail	10
Blue Moon Cocktail	10
Boston Bullet	12

Boston Cocktail	12
Bronx Cocktail	18
Bronx Cocktail (Dry)	18
Bronx Golden Cocktail	18
Bronx Silver Cocktail	18
Bronx Terrace	18
Brown Cocktail	18
Bulldog Cocktail	18
Bulldog Highball	18
Cabaret Cocktail	20
Café de Paris Cocktail	21
Casino Cocktail	22
Chelsea Side Car	23
Chocolate Soldier	24
Claridge Cocktail	25
Clover Club Cocktail	26
Clover Leaf Cocktail	26
Club Cocktail	26
Colonial Cocktail	26
Cooperstown Cocktail	28
Cornell Cocktail	28
Coronation Cocktail	28
Cream Fizz	28
Creme de Gin Cocktail	29
Crimson Cocktail	29
Crystal Slipper Cocktail	29
Damn-the-Weather	30
Darb Cocktail	30
Deep Sea Cocktail	30
Dempsey Cocktail	30
Diamond Fizz	31
Dillantini Cocktail	31
Dixie Cocktail	31
Double Standard Sour	32
Dry Martini Cocktail	117
DuBarry Cocktail	32
Dubonnet Cocktail	32
Eclipse Cocktail	33
Emerald Isle Cocktail	34
English Highball	34
English Rose	34
Fairy Belle Cocktail	36
Fallen Angel Cocktail	36
Fancy Gin Cocktail	36
Farmer's Cocktail	37
Favourite Cocktail	37
Fifty-Fifty Cocktail	37
Fine and Dandy	37
Flamingo Cocktail	38
Floradora Cooler	38
Fog Horn	38
Frankenjack Cocktail	38

141

French "75"	38	
Froth Blower	39	
Gibson Cocktail	117	
Gilroy Cocktail	39	
Gimlet Cocktail	40	
Gin and Bitters	40	
Gin and It (English)	40	
Gin and Tonic	40	
Gin Buck	40	
Gin Cobbler	40	
Gin Cocktail	40	
Gin Cooler	40	
Gin Daisy	40	
Gin Fix	40	
Gin Fizz	41	
Gin Highball	41	
Gin Milk Punch	41	
Gin Rickey	41	
Gin Sangaree	41	
Gin Sling	41	
Gin Smash	41	
Gin Sour	41	
Gin Squirt	43	
Gin Swizzle	43	
Gin Toddy	43	
Gin Toddy (Hot)	43	
Golf Cocktail	43	
Grand Royal Fizz	44	
Grapefruit Cocktail	44	
Green Dragon Cocktail	44	
Green Fizz	44	
Green Swizzle	44	
Gypsy Cocktail	44	
Harlem Cocktail	45	
Hasty Cocktail	45	
Hawaiian Cocktail	46	
Hoffman House	47	
Homestead Cocktail	47	
Honolulu No. 1	47	
Honolulu No. 2	47	
Hotel Plaza Cocktail	48	
H. P. W. Cocktail	48	
Hula-Hula Cocktail	48	
Ideal Cocktail	49	
Imperial Cocktail	49	
Income Tax Cocktail	49	
Jamaica Glow Cocktail	51	
Jewel Cocktail	52	
Jeyplak Cocktail	52	
Jockey Club Cocktail	52	
John Collins	52
Journalist Cocktail	52
Judge, Jr., Cocktail	52
Judgette Cocktail	52
K. C. B. Cocktail	53
Kiss-in-the-Dark	55
Knickerbocker Cocktail	55
Knock-Out Cocktail	55
Kup's Indispensable	55
Lady Love Fizz	56
Lasky Cocktail	56
Leap Frog Highball	56
Leap Year Cocktail	56
Leave It To Me No. 1	57
Leave It To Me No. 2	57
Little Devil Cocktail	59
London Buck Highball	59
London Cocktail	59
Lone Tree Cocktail	60
Lone Tree Cooler	60
Maiden's Blush	61
Major Bailey	61
Mamie's Sister	62
Manila Fizz	62
Martinez Cocktail	62
Martini (Dry)	116
Martini (Medium)	116
Martini (Sweet)	117
Maurice Cocktail	63
Melon Cocktail	63
Merry Widow No. 1	63
Million Dollar Cocktail	64
Mr. Manhattan Cocktail	65
Monte Carlo Highball	65
Montmartre Cocktail	65
Napolean Cocktail	67
Negronis	67
New Orleans Gin Fizz	67
North Pole Cocktail	68
Opal Cocktail	69
Opera Cocktail	69
Orange Blossom	69
Orchid Cocktail	71
Palm Beach Cocktail	71
Paradise Cocktail	72
Peach Blossom	72
Peach Blow Fizz	72
Peggy Cocktail	73
Perfect Cocktail	73
Peter Pan Cocktail	73
Piccadilly Cocktail	73
Pink Gin	74
Pink Lady Cocktail	74
Pink Pussy Cat	74
Pink Rose Fizz	74
Plaza Cocktail	76
Pollyanna Cocktail	76
Polo Cocktail	76
Poppy Cocktail	76
Prince's Smile Cocktail	78
Princeton Cocktail	78
Queen Elizabeth	79
Racquet Club Cocktail	80
Ramos Fizz	80
Red Swizzle	80
Remsen Cooler	80
Resolute Cocktail	81
Robert E. Lee Cooler	81
Rolls-Royce Cocktail	81
Roma Cocktail	81
Rose Cocktail (English)	82
Rose Cocktail (French)	82
Roselyn Cocktail	82
Royal Clover Club	82
Royal Cocktail	82
Royal Fizz	82
Royal Smile	82
Russian Cocktail	85
Salty Dog	86
Sand-Martin Cocktail	86
Sensation Cocktail	88
Seventh Heaven	88
Silver Cocktail	90
Silver Fizz	90
Silver King Cocktail	90
Silver Stallion Fizz	90
Singapore Sling	91
Smile Cocktail	92
Smiler Cocktail	92
Snowball Cocktail	92
Society Cocktail	92
South Side Cocktail	93
South Side Fizz	93
Southern Gin Cocktail	93
Spencer Cocktail	93
Sphinx Cocktail	93
Spring Feeling Cocktail	93
Stanley Cocktail	93

Star Daisy	95
Straight Law Cocktail	95
Sunshine Cocktail	95
Sweet Patootie	96
Tailspin Cocktail	96
Tango Cocktail	96
Thanksgiving Cocktail	97
Third Degree Cocktail	97
Three Stripes Cocktail	99
Thunderclap Cocktail	99
Tom Collins	100
Trinity Cocktail	100
Turf Cocktail	101
Tuxedo Cocktail	101
Twin Six Cocktail	101
Ulanda Cocktail	101
Union Jack Cocktail	101
Violet Fizz	103
Wallick Cocktail	105
Webster Cocktail	105
Wedding Belle Cocktail	105
Wembley Cocktail	106
Western Rose Cocktail	106
White Cargo Cocktail	109
White Lady Cocktail	109
White Lily Cocktail	109
White Rose Cocktail	109
White Way Cocktail	110
Xanthia Cocktail	110
Yale Cocktail	110
Zaza Cocktail	112

EGGNOGS

This is a most agreeable, enriching way of taking whole eggs and milk. They can be served in cups, from a bowl, at the holiday season or in a tall, individually prepared glass. In either case, a sprinkling of nutmeg is a must.

Ambassador's Morning Lift	115
Baltimore Eggnog	5, 115
Brandy Eggnog	14, 115
Breakfast Eggnog	17, 115
Christmas Yule Eggnog	24, 115
Cider Eggnog	24
General Harrison's Eggnog	39, 115
Imperial Eggnog	115
Nashville Eggnog	115
Port Wine Eggnog	77, 115
Rum Eggnog	84, 115
Sherry Eggnog	89, 115
Whiskey Eggnog	107, 115

FIXES

These sweet "miniature" Cobblers are made in highball glasses with liquor, lemon juice, sugar and lots of shaved ice. Serve with fruits, berries and straws.

Brandy Fix	14
Gin Fix	40
Rum Fix	84
Whiskey Fix	107

FIZZES

An early morning, midafternoon or evening pleasure, these are made from liquor, citrus juices and sugar, shaken with ice and strained into small highball glasses, which are then filled with "fizz" (soda) water, though different carbonated beverages, even Champagne, may be used. A few call for egg whites or yolks.

Alabama Fizz	2
Albemarle Fizz	2
Apple Blow Fizz	3
Apricot Fizz	4
Bird of Paradise Fizz	8
Brandy Fizz	14
Bucks Fizz	18
Cherry Fizz	23
Chicago Fizz	23
Cream Fizz	28
Derby Fizz	31
Diamond Fizz	31
Dubonnet Fizz	32
Gin Fizz	41
Golden Fizz	43
Grand Royal Fizz	44
Green Fizz	44
Imperial Fizz	49
Japanese Fizz	51
Lady Love Fizz	56
Manila Fizz	62
May Blossom Fizz	63
Merry Widow Fizz	63
Morning Glory Fizz	66
New Orleans Gin Fizz	67
Orange Gin Fizz	69
Orange Milk Fizz	71
Peach Blow Fizz	72
Pineapple Fizz	74
Pink Rose Fizz	74
Ramos Fizz	80
Royal Fizz	82
Ruby Fizz	82
Silver Fizz	90
Silver Stallion Fizz	90
Sloe Gin Fizz	91
South Side Fizz	93
Violet Fizz	103

FLIPS

This combination Eggnog and Fizz is made with liquor, egg and sugar, shaken well with cracked ice and strained into short-stemmed flip glasses. Good early-morning or bedtime drinks, sprinkled with nutmeg.

Brandy Flip	14
Cherry Flip	23
Chocolate Flip	24
Coffee Flip	26
Hot Brandy Flip	48
Ice Cream Flip	49
Port Wine Flip	77
Sherry Flip	89
Sloe Gin Flip	91
Whiskey Flip	107

Gin Drinks
(See Dry Gin Drinks, on page 141 of Index)

Highballs

These are all-time favorites and simple to make. Practically any liquor may be used, in combination with ice, soda or plain water, ginger ale and a host of other carbonated liquids.

Apple Brandy Highball	4
Bermuda Highball	8
Billie Taylor	8
Bitters Highball	9
Bourbon Highball	13
Brandy Highball	16
Bulldog Highball	18
Bull's Eye	20
Cablegram Highball	20
Cognac Highball	26
Cuba Libre	29
Dubonnet Highball	32
English Highball	34
Gin and Tonic	40
Gin Highball	41
Hill Billy Highball	47
Horse's Neck	47
Irish Whiskey Highball	50
Jamaica Granito	51
Leap Frog Highball	56
London Buck Highball	59
Mamie Gilroy	61
Mamie Taylor	61
Mexicola Highball	63
Mint Highball	64
Monte Carlo Imperial Highball	65
Orange Gin Highball	69
Rum Highball	84
Rye Highball	85
Scotch Whiskey	88
Spritzer Highball	93
Stone Fence	95
Susie Taylor	95
Vodka and Tonic	103
Whiskey Highball	107

Hot Drinks

Made right and served piping hot, these are fine drinks for snappy days and cold evenings. Don't use too much liquor in any hot drink; if it's too strong it can't be taken until it cools and then it's no good.

American Grog	3
Blue Blazer	10
Brandy Blazer	13
Brandy Toddy (Hot)	17
Café Royal	21
Gin Toddy (Hot)	43
Hot Brandy Flip	48
Hot Brick Toddy	48
Hot Buttered Rum	48
Hot Buttered Wine	48
Irish Coffee	49
Mulled Claret	66
Night Cap	68
Port Wine Negus	77
Rum Toddy (Hot)	85
Tom and Jerry	100
Whiskey Skin	108
Whiskey Toddy (Hot)	109

Irish Whiskey Drinks

Blarney Stone Cocktail	9
Cameron's Kick	21
Everybody's Irish	34
Irish Coffee	49
Irish Rickey	50
Irish Shillelagh	50
Irish Whiskey Cocktail	50
Irish Whiskey Highball	50
Paddy Cocktail	71
Rory O'More	82
St. Patrick's Day	86
Shamrock Cocktail	89
Tipperary Cocktail	100

Jamaica Rum Drinks
(Also see Rum Drinks on page 145)

Ambassador's Morning Lift	115
Baltimore Eggnog	5, 115
Chinese Cocktail	23
East India No. 1	33
Huntsman Cocktail	48
Jamaica Glow Cocktail	51
Modern Cocktail	65
Nashville Eggnog	115
Parisian Blonde Cocktail	72
Planter's Cocktail	74
Robson Cocktail	81
Shanghai Cocktail	89
Zombie	112

Juleps

Juleps come from Kentucky, but cool and refreshing anywhere. Traditionally made with Kentucky bourbon and fresh mint leaves (muddled, crushed or whole), these may be made with rye, brandy, gin, rum or champagne. Serve with shaved ice in an ice-frosted glass with mint or fruit garnish and straws.

Brandy Julep	16
Dixie Julep	31
Mint Julep	65
Mint Julep (Southern Style)	65

Kummel Drinks

Allies Cocktail	2
Green Dragon Cocktail	44
K. C. B. Cocktail	53
Tovarich Cocktail	100

Orange-Flavored Gin Drinks

Leap Year Cocktail	56
Orange Gin Collins	69
Orange Gin Fizz	69
Orange Gin Highball	69
Orange Gin Rickey	71
Orange Milk Fizz	71

Peach Brandy Drinks

Fish House Punch	37
Judgette Cocktail	52
Peach Sangaree	72

Pousse Cafés

These sweet, striped wonders are made from a series of cordials and liqueurs poured in succession so that one floats on another. Follow the recipes exactly to get the layers of ingredients in the right order. See "How To Float Cordials" in the Bar Hints section.

Angel's Delight	3
Angel's Kiss	3
Angel's Tip	3
Angel's Wing	3
Fifth Avenue	37
Port and Starboard	77
Pousse Café	77
Pousse L'Amour	78
Princess Pousse Café	78
Stars and Stripes	95

Punches

Perfect for parties, they can be mixed in endless variety. Cold punches usually contain citrus juices with two or more liquors or wines. Hot punches often use milk, eggs and cream as a base.

Banana Punch	7
Bombay Punch	12
Brandy Milk Punch	16
Brandy Punch	16
Brighton Punch	18
Cardinal Punch	21
Champagne Punch	22
Claret Punch	25
Fish House Punch	37
Gin Milk Punch	41
Glögg	43
Irish Shillelagh	50
Milk Punch	64
Planter's Punch No. 1	76
Planter's Punch No. 2	76
Port Milk Punch	77
Royal Purple Punch	82
Rum Milk Punch	85
Scotch Milk Punch	87
Sherry Milk Punch	89
Whiskey Milk Punch	108

Rickeys

A cross between a Collins and a Sour, they are always made with lime, cracked ice, soda water or some other carbonated beverage. The liquor may be whiskey, gin, rum or brandy. Serve with the rind of the lime left in the glass.

Apple Brandy Rickey	4
Apricot Brandy Rickey	4
Fog Horn	38
Gin Rickey	41
Grenadine Rickey	44
Irish Rickey	50
Orange Gin Rickey	71
Rum Rickey	85
Scotch Rickey	88
Sloe Gin Rickey	91
Twister	101
Whiskey Rickey	108

Rum Drinks

(Also see Jamaica Rum Drinks on page 144)

American Grog	3
Apple Pie Cocktail	4
Bacardi Cocktail	5
Banana Daiquiri	7
Barbary Coast Cocktail	7
Between the Sheets	8
Bolero Cocktail	10
Bolo Cocktail	12
Boston Cooler	12
Boston Side Car	12
Brown Cocktail	18
Burgundy Bishop	20
Bull's Milk	20
Cape Codder	21
Cardinal Punch	21
Chicago Fizz	23
Christmas Yule Eggnog	24, 115
Cream Puff	28
Cuba Libre	29
Cuban Cocktail No. 1	29
Cuban Cocktail No. 2	29
Cuban Special	29
Daiquiri Cocktail	30
El Presidente No. 1	33
El Presidente No. 2	33
Eyeopener Cocktail	34
Fair and Warmer	36
Fireman's Sour	37
Fish House Punch	37
Frozen Daiquiri	39
Havana Cocktail	45
Hop Toad Cocktail	47
Hot Buttered Rum	48
Imperial Fizz	49
Irish Shillelagh	50
Judge, Jr. Cocktail	52
Knickerbocker Special	55
Liberty Cocktail	59
Little Devil Cocktail	59
Little Princess Cocktail	59
Mai-Tai	61
Mary Pickford	62
Nevada Cocktail	67
Night Cap	68
Palmetto Cocktail	72
Passion Daiquiri	72
Pineapple Cocktail	73
Pineapple Fizz	74
Planter's Punch No. 1	76
Planter's Punch No. 2	76
Poker Cocktail	76
Quaker's Cocktail	79
Quarter Deck Cocktail	79
Rum Cobbler	84
Rum Cola	84
Rum Collins	84
Rum Cooler	84
Rum Daisy	84
Rum Eggnog	84, 115
Rum Fix	84
Rum Highball	84
Rum Milk Punch	85
Rum Rickey	85
Rum Sour	85
Rum Swizzle	85
Rum Toddy	85
Rum Toddy (Hot)	85
Santiago Cocktail	86
Saxon Cocktail	87
September Morn	88
Sevilla Cocktail	88
Sir Walter Cocktail	91
Sloppy Joe's No. 1	92
Spanish Town Cocktail	93
Stanley Cocktail	93
Stone Cocktail	95

Susie Taylor	95
Third Rail Cocktail	97
Three Miller Cocktail	99
Tom and Jerry	100
West Indies Frosted	106
White Lily Cocktail	109
White Lion Cocktail	109
X. Y. Z. Cocktail	110
Zombie	112

RYE WHISKEY DRINKS

(See Whiskey Drinks, on page 147 of Index)

SANGAREES

These are taller, sweet Old Fashioneds (without bitters); they may be made with whiskey, gin, rum or brandy, with port wine floated on top, or with wine, ale, porter or stout, with a sprinkle of nutmeg.

Brandy Sangaree	16
Gin Sangaree	41
Peach Sangaree	72
Port Wine Sangaree	77
Sherry Sangaree	90
Whiskey Sangaree	108

SCOTCH WHISKY DRINKS

Affinity Cocktail	1
Barbary Coast Cocktail	7
Beadlestone Cocktail	7
Beals Cocktail	7
Blood and Sand	9
Bobby Burns Cocktail	10
Cameron's Kick	21
Derby Fizz	31
Flying Scotchman	38
Harry Lauder Cocktail	45
Highland Cooler	46
Highland Fling	46
Hole-In-One Cocktail	47
Hoot Mon Cocktail	47
Mamie Gilroy	61
Mamie Taylor	61
Miami Beach Cocktail	64
Modern Cocktail	65
Morning Glory Fizz	66
Rob Roy Cocktail	81
Rusty Nail	85
Scotch Bishop Cocktail	87
Scotch Cooler	87
Scotch Milk Punch	87
Scotch Mist	88
Scotch Old Fashioned	88
Scotch Rickey	88
Scotch Sour	88
Scotch Stinger	88
Scotch Whisky Highball	88
Stone Fence Highball	95
Thistle Cocktail	97

SLINGS

These are like Sangarees, but made with the addition of lemon juice and a twist of lemon peel. Usually served in an Old Fashioned glass.

Brandy Sling	16
Cherry Sling	23
Gin Sling	41
Singapore Sling	91
Vodka Sling	104
Whiskey Sling	108

SLOE GIN DRINKS

Black Hawk Cocktail	9
Chocolate Flip	24
Clove Cocktail	25
Eclipse Cocktail	33
Irish Shillelagh	50
Johnnie Cocktail	52
Lemonade (Modern)	59
Love Cocktail	60
McClelland Cocktail	63
Merry Widow Fizz	63
Moulin Rouge Cocktail	66
Ping-Pong Cocktail	74
Ruby Fizz	82
San Francisco	86
Shriner Cocktail	90
Sloeberry Cocktail	91
Sloe Driver	91
Sloe Gin Cocktail	91
Sloe Gin Collins	91
Sloe Gin Fizz	91
Sloe Gin Flip	91
Sloe Gin Rickey	91

SMASHES

These are junior-sized Juleps served in Old Fashioned glasses. Make with muddled sugar, ice cubes and whiskey, gin, rum or brandy as well as sprigs of mint and a squirt of soda water, if desired, and garnish with fruit.

Brandy Smash	17
Gin Smash	41
Whiskey Smash	108

SOURS

Made with lemon juice, ice, sugar and any of the basic liquors, these are tart lemon-y cocktails similar to a highly concentrated Punch. Decorate with a lemon slice and cherry.

Apple Brandy Sour	4
Boston Sour	13
Brandy Sour	17
Double Standard Sour	32
Egg Sour	33
Fireman's Sour	37
Frisco Sour	39
Gin Sour	41
New York Sour	67
Rum Sour	85
Scotch Sour	88
Sourteq	92
Tequila Sour	97
Vodka Sour	104
Whiskey Sour	108

SWEDISH PUNCH DRINKS

Biffy Cocktail	8
Lasky Cocktail	56
May Blossom Fizz	63

146

Swizzles

These drinks originally came from the West Indies where a swizzle stick is a twig having three to five forked branches on the end; it is inserted into the glass or pitcher and twirled rapidly between the hands. Tall, cool drinks of lime, sugar, liquor, bitters and packed with shaved ice.

Brandy Swizzle	17
Gin Swizzle	43
Green Swizzle	44
Red Swizzle	80
Rum Swizzle	85
Whiskey Swizzle	109

Tequila Drinks

Margarita Cocktail	62
Mexicola	63
Sourteq	92
Tequila Collins	97
Tequila Sour	97
Tequila Straight	97
Tequini Cocktail	97, 117
Tequonic	9

Toddies

These may be served hot or cold. Dissolve a lump or teaspoon of sugar in a little water. Add liquor, ice or hot water and stir with clove, nutmeg, cinnamon or lemon peel.

Brandy Toddy	17
Brandy Toddy (Hot)	17
Gin Toddy	43
Gin Toddy (Hot)	43
Hot Brick Toddy	48
Hot Buttered Rum	48
Pendennis Toddy	73
Rum Toddy	85
Rum Toddy (Hot)	85
Whiskey Toddy	109
Whiskey Toddy (Hot)	109

Triple Sec Drinks

Angel's Delight	3
Between the Sheets	8
Blue Monday	10
Boston Side Car	12
Champagne Cup	22
Chelsea Side Car	23
Cider Cup	24
Claret Cup	25
Claridge Cocktail	25
Deauville Cocktail	30
Duke Cocktail	32
Fine and Dandy	37
Frankenjack Cocktail	38
Little Devil Cocktail	59
Loving Cup	60
Margarita Cocktail	62
Montmartre Cocktail	65
Opal Cocktail	69
Rhine Wine Cup	81
Sauterne Cup	87
Scotch Bishop Cocktail	87
Sherry Twist Cocktail	90
Side Car Cocktail	90
Ulanda Cocktail	101
White Lily Cocktail	109
X. Y. Z. Cocktail	110

Vodka Drinks

Banana Punch	7
Black Magic	9
Black Russian	9
Bloody Bloody Mary	10
Bloody Mary Cocktail	10
Blue Monday Cocktail	10
Cape Codder	21
Clam & Tomato Cocktail	25
Flying Grasshopper	38
Headless Horseman	46
Huntsman	48
Kangaroo Cocktail	53
Kretchma Cocktail	55
Moscow Mule	66
Ninitchka Cocktail	68
Pink Pussy Cat	74
Polynesian Cocktail	76
Russian Bear Cocktail	85
Russian Cocktail	85
Screwdriver	88
Tovarich Cocktail	100
Twister	101
Vodka and Apple Juice	103
Vodka and Tonic	103
Vodka Bloody Mary	103
Vodka Collins	103
Vodka Cooler	104
Vodka Daisy	104
Vodka Gibson Cocktail	117
Vodka Gimlet Cocktail	104
Vodka Grasshopper	104
Vodka Gypsy Cocktail	104
Vodka Martini Cocktail	117
Vodka on the Rocks	104
Vodka "7"	104
Vodka Sling	104
Vodka Sour	104
Vodka Stinger	104
Vodkatini	117

Whiskey Drinks

(Bourbon, Blended, Rye or Canadian)

Ambassador's Morning Lift Eggnog	115
Black Hawk Cocktail	9
Blue Blazer	10
Boston Sour	13
Bourbon Highball	13
Brighton Punch	18
Cablegram Highball	20
California Lemonade	21
Christmas Yule Eggnog	24, 115
Commodore Cocktail	28
Cowboy Cocktail	28
Creole Lady Cocktail	29
Dinah Cocktail	31
Dixie Julep	31
Dixie Whiskey Cocktail	31
Double Standard Sour	32
Elk's Own Cocktail	34
Fancy Whiskey Cocktail	36
Fox River Cocktail	38
Frisco Sour	39
Horse's Neck	47
Hot Brick Toddy	48
Imperial Fizz	49
Japanese Fizz	51
Kentucky Cocktail	53
Kentucky Colonel	53
King Cole Cocktail	53
Klondike Cooler	55
Ladies' Cocktail	56
Lawhill Cocktail	56
Linstead Cocktail	59

Los Angeles Cocktail	60
Manhattan Cocktail	62
Manhattan (Dry)	62
Manhattan (Sweet)	62
Milk Punch	64
Millionaire Cocktail	64
Mint Julep	65
Mint Julep (Southern Style)	65
Mountain Cocktail	66
Nashville Eggnog	115
New York Cocktail	67
New York Sour	67
Old Fashioned Cocktail	68
Old Pal Cocktail	68
Opening Cocktail	69
Oriental Cocktail	71
Palmer Cocktail	72
Pendennis Toddy	73
Preakness Cocktail	78
Rattlesnake Cocktail	80
Rye Highball	85
Rye Whiskey Cocktail	85
Sazerac Cocktail	87
Soul Kiss Cocktail	92
Swiss Family Cocktail	96
Temptation Cocktail	96
Thunderclap Cocktail	99
T. N. T. Cocktail	100
Trilby Cocktail	100
Ward Eight	105
Whiskey Cobbler	106
Whiskey Cocktail	106
Whiskey Collins	106
Whiskey Daisy	106
Whiskey Eggnog	107, 115
Whiskey Fix	107
Whiskey Flip	107
Whiskey Highball	107
Whiskey Milk Punch	108
Whiskey Orange	108
Whiskey Rickey	108
Whiskey Sangaree	108
Whiskey Skin	108
Whiskey Sling	108
Whiskey Smash	108
Whiskey Sour	108
Whiskey Squirt	108
Whiskey Swizzle	109
Whiskey Toddy	109
Whiskey Toddy (Hot)	109
Whispers of the Frost	109
White Plush	109

WILD CHERRY BRANDY DRINKS

Blood and Sand	9
Bulldog Cocktail	18
Cherry Blossom	23
Cherry Fizz	23
Cherry Flip	23
Cherry Sling	23
Dubonnet Fizz	32
Gilroy Cocktail	39
Kiss-in-the-Dark	55
Merry Widow No. 2	63
Polynesian Cocktail	76
Rose Cocktail (French)	82
Singapore Sling	91
Vanderbilt Cocktail	103
Wedding Belle Cocktail	105
Xanthia Cocktail	110

WINE DRINKS

Claret, Madeira, Muscatel, Port, Rhine, Sauterne, Sherry, White wine

(See Champagne Drinks on page 139)

Adonis Cocktail	1
American Beauty	3
Baltimore Eggnog	5, 115
Bamboo Cocktail	5
Bishop	8
Bombay Punch	12
Brandy Sangaree	16
Brazil Cocktail	17
Broken Spur Cocktail	18
Burgundy Bishop	20
Cardinal Punch	21
Chicago Fizz	23
Chocolate Cocktail	24
Chocolate Daisy	24
Claret Cobbler	25
Claret Cup	25
Claret Punch	25
Clove Cocktail	25
Coffee Cocktail	26
Coffee Flip	26
Creole Lady Cocktail	29
Crimson Cocktail	29
Devil's Cocktail	31
East India No. 2	33
Elk's Own Cocktail	34
General Harrison's Eggnog	39, 115
Gin Sangaree	41
Glögg	43
Hot Buttered Wine	48
Hot Springs Cocktail	48
Jamaica Glow Cocktail	51
Japanese Fizz	51
Lemonade (Modern)	59
Loving Cup	60
Mint Gin Cocktail	64
Mulled Claret	66
Peach Sangaree	72
Pineapple Cooler	73
Poop Deck Cocktail	76
Port Milk Punch	77
Port Wine Cobbler	77
Port Wine Cocktail	77
Port Wine Eggnog	77, 115
Port Wine Flip	77
Port Wine Negus	77
Port Wine Sangaree	77
Quarter Deck	79
Queen Charlotte	79
Reform Cocktail	80
Rhine Wine Cup	81
Rock & Rye Cocktail	81
Royal Purple Punch	82
Sauterne Cup	87
Sevilla Cocktail	88
Sherry and Egg Cocktail	89
Sherry Cobbler	89
Sherry Cocktail	89
Sherry Eggnog	89, 115
Sherry Flip	89
Sherry Milk Punch	89
Sherry Sangaree	90
Sherry Twist Cocktail	90
Sloppy Joe's No. 2	92
Spritzer Highball	93
Stone Cocktail	95
Straight Law Cocktail	95
Tempter Cocktail	96
Whiskey Sangaree	108
Whispers of the Frost	109
Xeres Cocktail	110

Product Illustrations

		Page
Straight Whiskies:	Bronze Label Kentucky Straight Bourbon	11
	Kentucky Spot Straight Bourbon	19
	Botled-in-Bond Kentucky Straight Bourbon	51
Blended Whiskies:	Rocking Chair Kentucky Whiskey—A Blend	ix, 46
	Pinch Blended Whiskey	15
	Deluxe Blended Whiskey	70
Imports:	Canadian Whisky	27
	Scotch Whiskies	35, 83
	Virgin Island Rum	42
Gins:	English Market Distilled Dry Gin	6
	Deluxe Distilled Dry Gin	54
	Sloe Gin, Mint and Orange Flavored Gins	58
Vodkas:	Vodka	75
Brandies:	Five Star Brandy	94
	Flavored Brandies	98
	Ginger Flavored Brandy	99
Cordials:	Creme de Menthe, Creme de Cacao Anisette, Kummel	102
Specialties:	Eggnog	107
	Peppermint Schnapps, Rock & Rye	111

Decorate with Labels

In response to many requests, Old Mr. Boston now offers a variety of colorful liquor labels for use in decorating waste baskets, lamp shades, screens, room dividers, trays, table tops, home bars and other such articles. All labels are genuine, have been printed in many colors, some on gold and silver foil paper. Many are embossed and several are die-cut into attractive, interesting shapes.

For a package of 30 different labels, in a variety of sizes, complete with illustrated instructions, send $1.00 to Decorating Labels, Old Mr. Boston, Boston 18, Mass.

Pearl-White Pourer

Illustrated on page 46. Safe, practical and washable, they screw on, have no corks to crumble, stick or replace. Interchangeable on all Old Mr. Boston fifths and quarts. 25¢ each from Pourer, Old Mr. Boston, Boston 18, Mass.

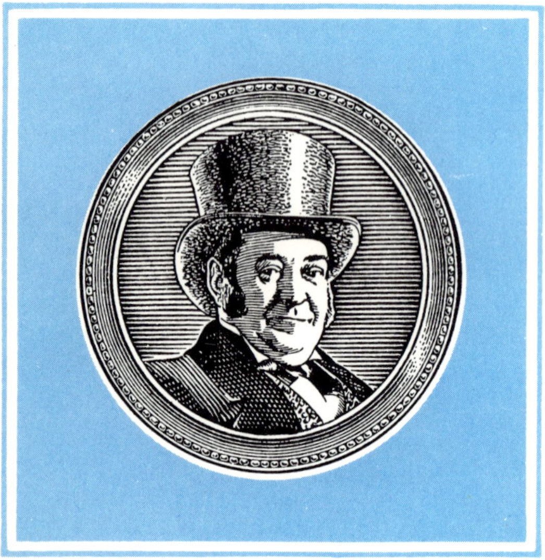

Port   Beer Goblet   Pony

Delmonico   Sherry   Whiskey Sour   Whiskey   Highball   Old Fashioned

Saucer Champagne   Cocktail   Cordial   Fizz   Stem   Rhine Wine   Brandy Inhaler